The Metaverse: A

An expert's guide to augmented reality (. technologies

by
Tom Ffiske

Acknowledgements
To coffee, which fueled my life and helped me finish this book.

How to read this book:

Welcome to *The Metaverse: A Professional Guide!* The book is designed so that you can hop to whichever chapter you wish to learn more about – just flick through the contents page, and consider where you want to start. Think of it as a choose-your-own-adventure book.

At times, it will feel like the topics bounce around. It is meant to be read at your own pace, where you decide to choose the parts you wish to look into. I believe in conciseness, and I hope you find the information you want as swiftly as you desire. Though of course, you can read it in any way you please.

Want to read from beginning to end? Go for it! Want to read the beginning and end so you sound smart at dinner parties? That works too, though be careful when the guests start asking questions. Want to read a few pages and then leave it on the shelf for a few years? We've all done that, so why not. There is a word for it: tsundoku, the art of buying books and not reading them.

Finally, you will see a scattering of references that either substantiate claims or have small bits of info that I couldn't fit in the book proper. Think of it as a friend that whispers something in your ear during a talk, with some helpful insights or comments on the side.[1]

Whichever path you choose, I hope you enjoy it!

---

[1] If you have ever read the *Bartimaeus Trilogy,* you will understand what I mean.

Contents

Preface – How the metaverse coincides with immersive technologies

Have you ever been confused by conversations around the metaverse? You are not alone. If you have been *frustrated* by the conversations, I can assure you that you are not alone, too.

Ever since the spike in interest during 2021, thousands of companies and pseudo-professionals ruffled through their websites and strapped the word to as many of their marketing materials as possible, capitalising on an explosion of interest. Suddenly, companies that hosted private virtual worlds are building towards a metaverse, or AR companies are mapping out the world to build it out. A comparable situation happened in 2017 when Bitcoin exploded in value and 'blockchain' was bolted on the side of new start-ups seeking venture funding.

Not all of these companies are providing substantial contributions to the discussions. The worst cases are companies that see they have a private world, and label it as a metaverse. The conversation will become nuanced over 2022 and beyond, but currently, it is a rush of companies identifying a new business opportunity.

If you ask any of these companies what the metaverse is, you will get a range of different answers.[2] Some say it is a super internet where

---

[2] You will also see companies who label it as a Metaverse with a big M. While the linguistic evolution of the term may

people can access experiences, zipping through the metaverse and going surfing, climbing, socialising and more. Others say it is a wholly social experience, where friends can hang out and conduct activities together. Still, others see it as a layer of reality, not a separate one: an overlay of information as people walk around the world. The madness of the conversations stems from the myriad of conversations that clutter social and mainstream media, obfuscating the view with a pyramid of poor takes.

My favourite definition comes from Matthew Ball, an established essayist who has been following the space more than the futurists in Silicon Valley bars: 'The metaverse is an expansive network of persistent, real-time rendered 3D worlds and simulations that support continuity of identity, objects, history, payments, and entitlements, and can be experienced synchronously by an effectively unlimited number of users, each with an individual sense of presence.'[3] A wide definition that covers many different technologies – hence the confusion on what the metaverse will look like.

One other factor, less touched-on, is that our conception of the metaverse is based on our modern-day perception of tech. We see it as an evolution of the internet, an inevitability as we continue to evolve its function. But is that

flow towards the capitalised M, I will opt for the alternative.
[3] 'Framework for the Metaverse.' MatthewBall.VC https://www.matthewball.vc/all/forwardtothemetaverseprimer. Accessed 22 Jan. 2022.

necessarily what it will look like? Our present influences how we view the future, like a lens that warps what the next few years will truly look like. A later chapter will use an example from a 1900s chocolatier predicting the 2000s, with visions of cities on trains or wooden flying machines. The metaverse will go beyond our conceptions today and dabble into use-cases that we cannot predict.[4] The best we can do is to see what people want and build around what they truly desire.

Last thought before we dive in; be careful about the metaverse and what people say about it. Certainty lacks the flexibility of curious optimism. Observe, and build towards what you believe.

I hope this book provides some insights from my own experiences which will help you build your future. Welcome to your journey.

For many, NFTs are as tied to the metaverse as remoras with manta rays. I touch on the topic, but readers may be surprised about my cynicism. I understand why companies *want* to bring them together in discussions with the metaverse,[5] but the practice is misleading at best and fraudulent at worst.

---

[4] A more recent example; did anyone expect people to be paying hundreds of thousands of dollars for JPEGS in 2021? I understand why, but try pointing towards anyone who predicted the evolution with complete certainty.

[5] See: money

I'm aware that the above statement will compel some readers to close the book. The hype and excitement behind NFTs are bringing together a close-knit group of people who are collectively excited for the community and can artfully avoid rug pulls and back exciting projects. But my opposition against NFTs is that the majority are financially-motivated projects that lack wider value, and that some espouse a metaverse alignment when they do not. I do think NFTs could have value in a potential metaverse, just not now.

My distaste for NFTs stems from the definition of the metaverse; an interoperable place where users can converse, trade, and transfer themselves and goods across multiple locations. Today, we do not have many projects that fit the definition. Perhaps VRChat or Roblox, where avatars can transition from world to world–but most companies are effectively hosting their virtual servers. If a skin in *World of Warcraft* can transfer to Fortnite, then we have a macro-metaverse. Otherwise, it's high walls and a micro-metaverse. By the definition that some companies are using today, *Second Life* is a metaverse.[6]

But on paper, and long into the future, NFTs could work with a metaverse. They are already making waves in fashion: shoppers can buy a unique item, receive a certificate of

---

[6] It isn't, though I had a great conversation with Second Life players on how it set the foundations of what came in the decades afterwards.

ownership, then wear the item proudly in places like VRChat. The item can be one of only a few hundred copies, and it is unique to the wearer across a server. That scarcity and perceived value help to give it legitimacy in a virtual location.[7] I appreciate that the lack of scarcity is a good thing for many people, but having an artificial kind is important for certain objects to have value.

But in practice, it means nothing. The certificate is simply an entry on the blockchain, while the actual item could be used by anyone. It's like owning the receipt that proves you bought a watermelon but then seeing thousands of people eating them while chilling on the beach. The fundamental technology doesn't stop anyone from using the item themselves; it's more of a stamp of ownership which many won't acknowledge or legitimise. And worse, it doesn't work across multiple locations, as a metaverse should; oftentimes it works in very niche titles like VRChat, but nothing wider.

Fundamentally, brands are marketing a metaverse when it doesn't exist yet. The real metaverse will come in many years and will look nothing like we are seeing today. The experience of buying virtual items is just that – items locked in a small area of cyberspace. It is

---

[7] 'Luxury Fashion Brands Are Already Making Millions in the Metaverse.' Bloomberg.
https://www.bloomberg.com/news/articles/2021-12-09/luxury-fashion-brands-are-already-making-millions-in-the-metaverse Accessed 22 Jan. 2022.

telling that metaversenews.com only talks about NFTs, rather than, you know, the metaverse. I hope that the field will develop enough to step away from NFTs and focus on a more constructive and substantial view of the future.

I did not expect my expertise in virtual and augmented reality to lend a hand to the creation of this book. My previous book, *The Immersive Reality Revolution*,[8] explored the power and potential of immersive technologies across a range of industries. Now we are seeing one example of virtual reality's potential: its use with the metaverse. Originally this book was going to focus entirely on immersive technologies again, but with an evolved perspective.[9] But with the emergence of the metaverse, and how natural a fit it is with the conversation, I felt it was right to merge them and provide a comprehensive overview on the metaverse.

---

[8] 'The Immersive Reality Revolution Is Published.' Immersive Wire, 27 Feb. 2020, https://www.immersivewire.com/immersive-reality-revolution/.

[9] The title would have been the *Immersive Reality Revelation*, and the third book would have been the *Immersive Reality Declaration*. The trio's name would have been a pun on a line from the musical Hamilton, where one of the Schuyler Sisters sing 'You want a revolution? I want a revelation, so listen to my declaration.' I was incredibly close to writing three books and pulling off a Hamilton joke in the process.

Throughout the book, you will find that I talk about VR and AR, as well as their continued development about the metaverse. My central view is that these immersive technologies will be a part of the metaverse in the future in some form or another – but it is too early to say how. Like trees sprouting from the grounds of the Amazon rainforest, it is too early to say which sprouts soar towards the sky and which will shrivel and die. I hope to provide an overview of both technologies and provide my views on whether they can evolve to be a part of the metaverse.

My expertise spans five years of reading and writing about immersive technologies and their related topics.[10] I started *Virtual Perceptions* in 2016, spurred by the vibrant technology scene in London. The site evolved over the years and I published my first book in 2020, a bestseller in Amazon within the Virtual Reality category. Since then I started a weekly newsletter called the *Immersive Wire*, which delivers weekly insights into people's inboxes. The project became more popular than the site that birthed it, and I retired the *Virtual Perceptions* label in mid-2021 to focus fully on the *Immersive Wire*. The project sat alongside my work as a PR professional, where I helped companies raise their profile and clarify their messaging.

---

[10] I normally feel uncomfortable displaying my achievements, but I hope it brings some level of trust in what I say throughout the book.

Up to then, I was a passionate blogger who attended events and spoke to people across the industry – but a change came in early 2020 when I pivoted towards freelance work for a period and specialised in my newsletter. Since then I have been interviewed by national papers on immersive technologies, labelled by The Drum as a 'VR and AR marketing expert' and 'metaverse expert,'[11] and helped a range of companies with their communications efforts. I worked in-house for Zappar for a couple of years, helped the *London Film Festival's* immersive tech section of the activity in 2020, and aided groups like *Smash Drums!* announce their titles. I delivered the opening keynote for the *VRARA Global Summit* in 2021 and hosted panels exploring the metaverse during *VRDays Europe* the same year. Every day I receive news about companies developing new and exciting projects, and speak to university students who are quietly building astonishing projects. My specialism is in the realm of perception and communications, and I have a deep understanding that words can both reflect and shape reality.

I understand the area well, and I hope to be a safe pair of guiding hands through the book. But I must also declare my weaknesses as

---

[11] 'What's behind Big Tech's Rush to Launch AR Products for Retail Brands?' The Drum, https://www.thedrum.com/news/2021/08/19/what-s-behind-big-tech-s-rush-launch-ar-products-retail-brands. Accessed 22 Jan. 2022.

teacher, or other traditional methods. But as a complementary measure, AR can effectively teach concepts via immersion.

Or take retail. At the core of shopping is informing the customer on the product's qualities as best as possible before making a purchase. The more information they have, the more likely they will open their wallets and pay for a product. For years this meant working copy to be as informative as possible, targeting customer needs which the product can solve. Ever since the advent of online shopping, retail practices trended towards convenience and speed. In this sense, AR provides the next step. What better way of testing a product than seeing it as part of the world around you? For example, shopping for a sofa becomes easier if it can be virtually placed in a living room before purchase, seeing if the patchwork matches the wallpaper or what the view of the TV might be from the sofa once it's in the space.

There's no clearer example than try-on clothing. ASOS implemented AR with their shopping, letting people see their clothing in a unique way, before the items are delivered. Past text on a webpage, images on a screen, or videos providing a 360-degree view of a location, AR is the next iterative step for retailers.

Beyond shopping on the high street, AR might help tourism as well. Imagine visiting a location without leaving the house? Seeing the

---

https://www.immersivewire.com/curiscope-multiverse-posters/.

sloping inclines of the Alps, the white sands of Croatia, or the rainforests of the Amazon? As immersive technologies grew in sophistication, many companies grew excited about the potential for tourism. But having said that, interest waned to a trickle of interest. Very few activities in life can match the real adventure. No amount of technology can replicate the soft heat of the Caribbean sun, or the heated smell of nature in Jamaica. The future of augmented reality in tourism is nebulous because businesses no longer see the value of immersion in an activity where authenticity is key.

But my favourite area is marketing, which we will explore later in the book. Above all other industries, marketing is one of the most exciting areas for AR because it sits alongside other channels for reaching consumers. Social media helps shoppers keep track of a product's buzz. Television ads improve a brand's perception or messaging. Newsletters connect directly to engaged shoppers and help companies nurture their already-established relationships. AR sits alongside these measures for one reason: engagement. Here, 'augmented marketing' becomes powerful.

Companies can prove that a customer is engaged with a brand via their interactions with an AR experience, showing a direct relationship between interest and intention. The analytics can be collected and used in the future and are more powerful than a simple 'like' on Twitter or Facebook. Immersive experiences also lead to development would grow, or what might happen in the shifting patterns of consumer habits.

All I recommend at this stage is to keep an eye on both VR and AR as they grow, and see how they tie into the metaverse. Observe both as they develop further, and follow where the innovation and consumer interest flows. Both can form a part of the metaverse; it's a question of to what extent they'll do so, which only time will tell.

Key takeaways:
- Virtual reality (VR) is an immersive technology popularised by gaming, but with wider benefits across education and training.
- Hardware is getting cheaper and cheaper, with the standalone versions of VR headsets likely to stay in the long-term. The development of hardware is slow but steady, and we may see AR glasses this decade.
- Augmented reality (AR) is an overlay of the real world where people can play games or receive contextually relevant information.
- While it is difficult to pin down how AR and VR might contribute to the metaverse, following consumer interest will provide hints on where the flow of innovation may go.

Hopping through the metaverse

One frustration with discussions on the metaverse – as I am sure you will agree – is the absolute lack of clarity on the topic. The word encompasses everything and nothing: an internet of experiences; the next evolution of the internet. Anyone peering in may feel like they have an idea of what the metaverse is, but their conception will likely think differently from the next person's.

Ahead of this book, I asked my friends and family how they define it. All of them had different answers, with one friend astutely remarking that 'it is all hogwash'. The perspective is a shame, because the field has a lot of potential – it is just mired by a tide of incessant rubbish. Why should someone look into such a vague and nebulous area, one which can be described as hyper-capitalist because of its current link with NFTs? Why discuss something that does not technically exist yet?[21]

My answer is the same as what you may be thinking, and the reason you picked up this book. While we're in an early stage, the metaverse has the potential to impact multiple industries and the way we communicate with

---

[21] For a great critique of the metaverse, check out Adam Shepherd's opinion piece on the topic: 'The Metaverse Is a Waste of Time, Effort and Processing Power.' IT PRO, https://www.itpro.co.uk/business-strategy/collaboration/362032/metaverse-waste-of-time-effort-and-processing-power. Accessed 22 Jan. 2022.

each other. Though vague and indistinct as of yet, I believe the metaverse will evolve and solidify into a shape that will influence all of our lives. If you are as curious as I am, then it is important to track this evolution and spy on how early developments could feed into the journey. As Kimberly Shatzer from Onward Play said to me, 'The honest truth is that they are all stuck in "figuring it out" mode laying the railroad tracks while driving the train. The biggest request from clients exploring the metaverse space is, "Do you have any metaverse people?'

One quirk of the discussion is that it is also a linguistic battle; one where multiple participants are ironing out their definitions and splattering them across the internet until a cohesive one sticks. The most enthusiastic chatter seeps from all over the web, and the hype will settle into a cooler stance soon. Right now we're seeing the baying waves of discussions, as people reel to and fro between discussions and formulate what the metaverse might turn out to be. Keep in mind that a lot of the hard work has already been done, and there is already a wealth of information to learn more about the topic.

What's vital is that no one knows what the metaverse will look like. Most established professionals agree that we don't know entirely how the first version of the metaverse will work in practice, but there is a consensus on which principles will underline its future. The difference is that some design principles will be more valued than others; on my side, I hope for interoperability, perhaps over an OpenXR standard or an alternative, using open protocols that are not walled in.[22] Suzan Oslin, Program Manager for Spatial Experiences for Open AR Cloud, is working towards open standards as well: 'It's vital that there be a shared understanding of a universal coordinate system in order to provide a continuous user experience. Creating a common language that allows all metaverse service and content providers to play equally, i.e. interoperability, as well as providing safety and control to the user, is at the core of... [our] mission.'

The benefit of being at the inception of a new industry is that we have the power to shape it as we like. I don't want to sound like an anime protagonist, but the future is truly ours for the taking. And the next right step is to ensure we cut the bull, share good-quality information, and ride the train.

In 1900, a German chocolate factory named Theodor Hildebrand & Son released a series of postcards outlining their vision of the 21st century. Titled 'Germany in the year 2000,' the postcards showed trains pulling houses and towns on tracks, people flying with winged contraptions, and families floating through the air

---

[22] 'Chronos XR Standards'.
https://www.khronos.org/assets/uploads/developers/prese ntations/Khronos-XR-Standards-Laval-Virtual-Apr20.pdf.
Accessed 22 Jan. 2022.

The sentiment is hopeful, but still difficult to picture. Any company building the metaverse will want a significant stake in its use and control. Asking companies to collaborate to build a singular metaverse, where they all share in its success, would be difficult to follow and maintain, and completely antithetical to the way they currently conduct themselves and to our current global system of financial motivation. It is almost certain that some sort of government intervention may be needed to ensure how fair this balance is, especially as technological progress tends to surge faster than legal ramifications and systems of accountability. We lack the precedent for a cohesive policy, but the gap should at least be filled by a framework we all agree upon.

At the heart of the macro-metaverse concept is the tenet that much of the content would be created by users. Like the life of YouTube and other social media platforms, users create content that drives people towards engagement. The same will likely be true for the macro-metaverse, where people will hop into it to see the creations that users make and, subsequently, make money from. Roblox is a great example, where hundreds of users make a living from creating worlds on their platform. But again, I worry about how much of the pie companies would take if they hopped on the platform to sell their creations. And as much as

open-metaverse-requires-companies-to-have-enlightened-self-interest/.

it's an example of free-for-all creation, YouTube is also a platform rife with abuse and misinformation in need of moderation. All these pieces will come together to create a new macro-metaverse in the future, and this is about as much as is predictable. But the rest is in the air.

Like many, I am interested in seeing what the new metaverse will bring. A confluence of today's technologies will create a hodgepodge of new benefits which we can only speculate on today, based on the disparate pieces we can analyse. Many companies want to build the metaverse and become the go-to service providers for their infrastructure. If companies act or profess to act in 'enlightened self-interest,' we might think we can worry less. But any company with profit goals will always be tantalised to grab the opportunity and rake in the money as users become reliant on their services, and to prioritise that money above civic duties, environmental consequences, or global interests. If that happens, users will lose out. Companies will have many different versions of the metaverse in the future, confusing the dialogue further and competing with each other – hence why I differentiate above between several micro-metaverses and one macro-metaverse. The great prize is the latter, but riches will be made in the former.

I will chart the development in this field and track where it moves. But unlike others, I do not expect the metaverse to arrive in the next three or five years: it will be decades of progress, guided by the technologies of today. Anyone who tries to give a full prediction of the future, rather than a small glimpse, will look like the people of our past drawing family sky-blimps in postcards.

Key takeaways:
- We cannot know what the metaverse will look like, but we are relatively certain it will be interoperable and interconnected.
- We cannot predict the future because our perceptions of the future are influenced by the technologies of today.
- There will be micro-metaverses, which are self-contained and with their own merits, and a single macro-metaverse where all activities will occur.
- The metaverse will take decades of progress, and will be guided by what people want.

NFTs and the metaverse: Some promise, but a long way to go

If you scan the media, you would think that thousands of companies are building their products and services for the metaverse, from large-scale development like Meta to bite-sized services from smaller start-ups.[30] A typhoon of business ideas whizz through Twitter, and VCs are seeing an influx of companies adding the word 'metaverse' to their marketing materials. Some of these ventures are legitimate, but most actors are jumping on the hype train and hoping for the best. The situation reminds me of the blockchain hype of 2017: companies shoved blockchain into their services in the hopes of raising more capital for their business, buoyed by the emerging tech trends and trying to prey on the gullibility of investors impressed by buzzwords and new technologies. Inevitably, most start-ups failed to live up to their promises.

We will see the same with the metaverse, but perhaps to a more severe degree. The blockchain has tangible uses and already exists, with self-evident benefits that people can see and – for the affluent few – possess. But the metaverse doesn't even exist yet, with a myriad of differing definitions and companies who are working within their versions of the metaverse.

---

[30] The piece appeared first on my Immersive Wire website, with some updates. I felt it was right to place it in my book as it ties so neatly into metaverse discussions.

The mish-mash of approaches is leading to confusion, particularly in the public eye where they are only just learning about the topic. So when we consider how NFTs and the metaverse – two of the most emergent trends of 2021 – can work together, then we enter a collective mess of opinions and speculation. Some leaders, like Alan Smithson of MetaVRse, are particularly buoyant: 'The ability for creators to get paid for subsequent resales of their art is too attractive… [and] will effectively shape how we transact in the metaverse.'

Predicting the trajectory and form of the metaverse is like wondering what the next ten years will look like; our ideas are fuzzy and ill-defined, with a lot of guesses thrown in for good measure. But what is reasonably clear is that, while the underpinning technology is strong, we still have a long way to go before it is viable and trustworthy enough for wider use. Rampant cases of fraud, lack of environmental credentials, and overvaluation of items have led to a bloated NFT space that is surfing up the Gartner Hype Curve before potentially tumbling into the Trough of Disillusionment. But if those issues can be sufficiently addressed and repaired, NFTs may provide a firm bedrock for how financial transactions can happen in a potential metaverse.

NFTs may well have some utility in a potential metaverse that conveys value to virtual objects and land. Decentraland has proven that it is possible to have a persistent virtual world and be able to convey the value of locations via tokens, which can then be bought and sold in a secondary market. The same is true for physical items: unique ones can be produced and purchased, adding additional value and bringing life to a secondary market as people buy and sell their wares. In a virtual location where item production can be limitless, NFTs and their artificial scarcity add the necessary supply constraints to grant value.

NFTs will likely act as virtual objects or assets, rather than the simple images they act like today. Instead of an image that is simply owned and admired by a user, the object can be used however they wish in the metaverse; a table here, or an ornament there. Even property could be bought, and the token acts as the ownership rights of the location. Here is the biggest difference with an NFT in the metaverse: the object will have an impact on a virtual world, instead of granting access or prestige as part of an insular community. Doug Thomson argued that NFTs are not dependent on artificial scarcity, and are more a way for communities to self-organise.[31] I disagree as they would have limited numbers in a potential metaverse, but understand the point that they can also be used as a way for communities to rally together.

---

[31] 'The Metaverse Is Beautiful and Light.' Out of Scope, 29 Sept. 2021, https://outofscope.bureauofbrightideas.com/the-metaverse-is-beautiful-and-light/.

With such a wide market, it is more important than ever to consider interoperability as a potential portion of the market size. If an NFT can be used across the internet, then its value can expand as well as its utility. If a mobile phone can be used across the UK and US, without walls, then its value is increased for people who like to explore outer reaches without additional logistical constraints.[32]

These same thoughts are corroborated by Nicole Lazzaro, President of XEODesign: 'A walled garden metaverse delivers less value than a free and open one. For example, consider how hard it is to remember what platform someone messaged you on. Think about how much time humanity saves if they could consolidate all their contacts and communication in one space without a pricey CRM subscription.'

Such a walled garden may be possible: a solo location where all activities take place, which cannot pass into other realms. The barriers are common and even desirable, to protect the users within the wall from harmful content or accessing less-than-desirable areas of a virtual world. But the current discussions in this area come down to the individual rights of users within virtual worlds, and how much the governing companies are willing – or even allowed – to give over time.

---

[32] The approach then raises the question of fees; would NFTs face fees for their use in different parts of the metaverse?

In the end, what will work best for the metaverse is what works for its users. Companies are not people: they are made up of people, and so are user bases. We are at such an early stage of its development that its shape and form are not yet defined, with basic elements still undecided. Matthew Ball, a venture capitalist with extensive expertise in the space, points out that blockchains might not be the right answer: 'The metaverse has very few, if any, required technologies or models. The Internet did not need to use TCP/IP, it could have used other protocols and standards. The question is which is best for the metaverse economy, for individual users, and developers.

'The enthusiasm for blockchain stems, in part, from the belief it is less subject to gatekeeping and shifts more profits to the developer and rights to the user, rather than intermediaries and platforms. That sort of model is likely to be healthiest for the metaverse economy and individuals within it – but it isn't yet clear that blockchain is the best specific answer.'

The topic comes back to a core point – are NFTs even necessary? Surely an agreement on the value of virtual objects, without it being linked to the blockchain, will suffice for a functioning economy? NFTs add the scarcity needed to confer value, but does the enforced dearth need to be linked to the blockchain? It certainly means that every purchase can be verified (but not enforced), but the ledger itself may not necessarily need to be part of a decentralised network.

Then again, the value of decentralised finances stems from their lack of central control, and how an item's value can ebb and flow without the direct control of one organisation. That lack of centrality, the core of the metaverse, is enviable for some. Yet the fine details of ownership are not defined. 'Digital property rights have not yet been solved,' said Matthew Scott Jones, co-founder of MetaFabrix. How can an NFT convey ownership when the very basis of ownership is not defined?

All of the above draws from a central idea that we have no idea what the metaverse will look like or who will govern its terms. These suppositions and suggestions are mere thoughts thrown into the churning bucket of online discourse, while the engineers and developers in the background are building the future. But of the items explored and pondered, one area I am confident on is that the metaverse will become customer-focused, with no 'forced' technologies on them. If NFTs are forced, and not easy for people to use or buy, then they will deflate and die.

The most successful metaverse will be a frictionless experience that will be seamless for its users to enter, where they can do as they wish and pay as they please. The customer-first approach helped giants like Amazon thrive, crafting user journeys that made it as easy as possible for packages to appear by their door, no matter what happens elsewhere in the supply chain to enable it. The same goes for Netflix, which created Open Connect so that their content can be delivered anywhere in the world seamlessly, without buffering or glitches.[33] The metaverse will be the same, using a matrix of underpinning technologies that will be almost invisible as users dance the night away.

The exceptions are aspects that are linked to the safety of spaces and individuals. Security systems should be in place in online arenas to protect people, raising necessary barriers to limit or prevent harm or at least signpost and enforce rules of engagement. But when it comes to facilitating trade and granting people to do what they wish, then the most seamless options will always win. Currently, NFTs are not a good fit for the metaverse because of the sheer range of issues linked to them. Changes will need to be made, as currently, NFTs are not ready for use.

The core three issues with NFTs that I want to touch on are gas fees, severe value volatility, and fraud. In short, gas fees for buyers are so severe that they impinge on the value transactions that make seamless purchases. Value volatility distils a sense of mistrust on

---

[33] 'About Netflix - How Netflix Works With ISPs Around the Globe to Deliver a Great Viewing Experience.' About Netflix, https://about.netflix.com/, https://about.netflix.com/en/news/how-netflix-works-with-isps-around-the-globe-to-deliver-a-great-viewing-experience. Accessed 22 Jan. 2022.

recently-purchased assets. And fraud impinges on the system as a whole, and NFTs will become less trusted as an item to purchase.

Let's start with gas fees, a cost where buyers pay to mint on the blockchain. The best equivalent for them is an added tax where a vendor adds a fee to facilitate the purchase. The rate is normally a percentage, linked to the value of the item itself, or a set amount no matter what the purchase. A good equivalent is Paypal, which has a set minimum to pay for the transaction cost up to £25 (£0.50), then percentages from a certain amount upwards. The simplicity and transparency help facilitate trade; a wildly fluctuating fee hinders the purchasing process as people are unaware of how much they have to pay or unwilling to explore a service without clear up-front fees. By comparison, the Ethereum blockchain can fluctuate so severely, between values of £100 or £200 and spiking beyond, that it halts the purchasing process. For easy access for payments for the vast majority of consumers, the fee should be countable in pennies.

Even after the purchase, the value can fluctuate drastically. As a hypothetical example, an NFT could be purchased for £1.50, sold for £100, sold again for £1,000, then rest at £500 for perpetuity. A simple example, although minor when compared to the larger projects in the market. If NFTs are to link to the metaverse, the value must not fluctuate so wildly; a sense of value stability is required for assets to be seen as safer purchases, with potentially incremental increases in value over time. Property prices come to mind as a relatively safe purchase with minimal market fluctuations. Volatility breeds mistrust.

Fraud contributes to the lack of trust as well. Projects crop up all the time promising the world before pulling the rug and sending the value of items collapsing. Established projects soar in value once they build trust, and they become hallmarks for good NFTs (such as Bored Ape Yacht Club). But the vast majority of NFTs are smaller purchases with a risk factor, where users shuffle money between accounts to artificially increase the value of items.

The negative environmental impact of NFTs is another reason for scepticism of their viability, and one reason why companies like Discord are stepping back from NFTs.[34] I mention it here as a sub-point, as the overall trend is that many users are becoming more and more conscious of the environment and are actively working to minimise the impact of their choices on the planet. If the trend changes or a new type of blockchain comes that solves the issues, then it is worth exploring further.

The crux of the issue was summarised by Ricardo Tucker, AR Engineer at TikTok and independent game developer: 'NFT technologies

---

[34] 'Discord Halts Cryptocurrency and NFT Plans Following User Backlash.' Verdict, 12 Nov. 2021, https://www.verdict.co.uk/discord-nfts-cryptocurrency-backlash/.

are, at best, a proof of concept for how digital ownership could work in the future, but what's on the table right now isn't offering a complete solution to that problem.'

With the above in mind, here are my suggestions for how NFTs need to adjust to being a better fit for the metaverse:

- **Lower gas fees to set amounts**. No asset can have stability when the costs of transactions, though necessary, can fluctuate to severe degrees. For the majority of shoppers who want to buy virtual items, the fees must be measured in pennies.
- **Lower value volatility**. The process may naturally happen over time, as the market's bubble pops and the objects have a tangible use case in a virtual world. A virtual table does not need to vary in value so much, for example. But if it continues to fluctuate so severely, then fewer people will buy an NFT.
- **Combat fraud.** No project can ever have public trust alongside high levels of fraud. The process may become self-corrective as objects in the metaverse are viewable, and assets can be purchased when necessary. But the point is that the levels of fraud need to turn sharply downwards to instil more trust.

The above implies that I am cynical about the future of NFTs. Not so. The underpinning value of the technology is sound, as it will be important to keep track of object ownership within the metaverse. If the metaverse avoids having a singular governing body, then it may benefit from a decentralised version of tracking the purchase of items. If it works well and consumers can shop seamlessly, then they can buy what they need where necessary.

The community is thriving, with many people that say 'gm' (good morning) and bounce ideas off each other, collaborating and making friends. Like any group of people, there are bad actors that profit from the misdirection of others – but otherwise, the impression I have is that current users are ready to defend NFTs and their potential.

But as of yet the details need to be ironed out, at least for the metaverse. Complexities on ownership and the facilitation of trade are necessary to address before NFTs can be trusted enough for wider use. But once resolved, I look forward to a future where I may lean back in my NFT armchair while browsing the paper, reading about how the Bored Ape Yacht Club continues to have parties on top of virtual skyscrapers.

Key takeaways:
- NFTs are only tangentially related to the metaverse.

- The NFT scene is so full of fraud that it is difficult to trust its activities, which leads to general instability.
- While the basic technology could translate to the metaverse, it needs further evolution before it can be treated seriously.

The right design principles for building immersive products

The more money that flows into the sector, the more tools that are created to help new people enter the fold. I have the coding capabilities of a wooden spoon, but I am also aware of low-code applications where anyone can pick up and make basic applications after a little self-teaching. Tools like Unity, ZapWorks, and Blippar offer a range of ways for developers to get started, with a wealth of materials and courses to kickstart the process. With that ease comes light barriers of entry for anyone to access.[35]

Professionals are finding the same, and companies have stepped forward to plug the gap in the market with some (profitable) courses. Meanwhile, other platforms provide no-code solutions which allow people to create experiences by stringing together templates. While basic, this model helps beginners get the first jump into the area and make some basic (but still effective) experiences, creating a hunger for more.

Why do I mention all this? What about making VR experiences with your voice? That's what Anything World is trying to do in giving

---

[35] A number of courses can be found online and in the community. Some are better than others, but I do not wish to endorse any in this book. If you have a contact in the industry, consider speaking to them and they can offer guidance.

the right design approach to reel customers in. But a few companies invert their priorities – and that is when the trouble begins.

A common issue in many businesses is that they do not understand their customers. They try to, of course – monitoring customer emails, interview some people, and conduct research into what they want. But some companies take what a customer wants, misinterpret it, and provide the wrong design.

A classic example is user experience, and what they first see when they see a company for the first time. I will use one example, stripping the company's name and details; but bear in mind that this is a VR software provider currently operating in the industry, and this is the first thing people see when they enter the website:

INTEGRATE YOUR WORK INTO A DISCOVERY MAP:
Great user experience
Bring Leads to CRM Systems
On-board your clients
Stream Webinars

---

[37] That said, rocket scientists are not necessarily more clever: 'Rocket Scientists and Brain Surgeons Aren't Necessarily More Clever - Study.' BBC News, 14 Dec. 2021. www.bbc.co.uk, https://www.bbc.com/news/science-environment-59647067.

INTEGRATE YOUR WORK INTO A DISCOVERY MAP:
Video Library Publisher
Book a demo

The first reaction of many browsers would be confusion. The first few seconds do not outline what they do, how they can help, and what kind of technology they provide to service the customer's needs. The company is deep within themselves, keen to talk about what they do rather than how they can help. But most importantly, I am unsure why I would need a discovery map, or even what it is; what is the need being tackled?

If I were to re-work the website, I would step out of the company's services and think about what the customer would want, and why they would use the VR software provider. What is the need that needs to be addressed? For the sake of argument, let us say it is to provide an online way of presenting a portfolio – an easy, clickable way to see what their portfolio includes. In which case, I would reword it as:

PROVIDE A SEAMLESS WAY TO PRESENT YOUR WORK ONLINE:
Our service allows your partners and audience to click through and see your wide portfolio of services, demonstrating your value to potential

Additional details can be added as a cascade effect on the website, filtering information by prioritising the most important details downwards via a cascade of relevancy. Address how the need can be solved, then pen down the details with the technology and services that would be used. Because ultimately, most customers do not care how it is solved; they just want the job done.

The key learnings can apply to all immersive technologies, and the metaverse as well. Many companies in immersive tech present themselves in the wrong way. Companies are so preoccupied with the services they provide, and the cutting-edge technology they use, that they lose sight of what their customers may want. Clients do not necessarily want to do something because it 'looks cool.'

As I said earlier, I am not proposing that this is an issue across all companies. Design thinking is a big area, and a few companies are having issues expressing themselves. But in my view, the issue is widespread enough to stall our pick-up of new clients. On one level it is a communications issue, as potential customers are unsure what a particular VR / AR or metaverse company may do or be able to help them. For others it is more fundamental, to misunderstand what their customers want and provide the wrong solution. For example, one other fundamental issue is feeling sick in VR. While companies are pushing how 'revolutionising' VR is, users are still feeling nauseous. We cannot sweep them away – how can we push technology when there is an issue that needs to be addressed?

We cannot go in blindly and ignore the evident issues; the best approach to address them as much as we can. So grab an outside, invite them behind your doors, and listen carefully to what they say. Pop your bubble, take the feedback to heart, and innovate aggressively. You will not regret it.

Key takeaways:
- Most immersive products need a healthy dose of design thinking throughout their creation.
- Keep in mind the friction that customers face, and the perks they wish to receive when designing a product.
- Do not shy away from the big questions - addressing them head-on is the key to success.
- Identify the latent needs of customers – the issues which they may not articulate – to help create a successful product.

The long-running ramifications of Covid-19

After exploring the design principles of immersive technologies, it makes sense to tap into how the pandemic influenced their development and evolution.

I know, I am tired of this pandemic as well. Sick of it, even. Like many, I closely followed the political movements of the 2020s and did what I could to protect friends and family, and by the beginning of 2021 I was an inert and tired man who wanted to pop to the pub and see friends.[38] Still, the long-running effects of the pandemic on business are palpable, and worth a discussion for the book. VR and AR companies adapted their strategies to take advantage of a changing paradigm, with mixed successes. Though these developments did not have a direct impact on metaverse discussions, they impacted the technologies that may influence its further development or how it may be used. Let's look at how.

Unless you hid under a large rock, the last two years have been a bit of a cluster. Countries closed their borders, marching their army onto the streets to regulate people leaving their homes and handle supply chains initially. The consequences were that more people worked

---

[38] Much of the first lockdown consisted of video games, sourdough bread, and crippling anxiety; a calorific cocktail for a few months.

from home; waking up, making coffee, working, and sleeping in the same building over and over again. People could not go to their shopping street, the cinema, restaurants, cafes, or anywhere else. Just a few square metres of life, condensed into one bundle.

That said, many people have been self-isolating socially for a few years, as the internet makes it easier to enjoy social activities from their homes. Online video games let people socialise and play together from their sofa, not the arcade. Some friends prefer to video-chat and talk about their day, rather than meet in the local shopping centre. Want to watch a movie? Head to someone else's home and switch on a live-streaming service, not go to the over-priced cinema down the road. Still, the enforced isolation became a collective trauma across multiple countries at the same time.

The societal shift negatively impacted the hospitality sector. The world economy shook, jobs were lost, and good companies will take years to recover. Yet it was also an opportunity for other companies to thrive. Microsoft Teams and Zoom saw a massive spike in use – alongside crashes as the world logs on their computers at the same time. Agencies specialised in organising online events thrived, as companies sought alternatives to physical gatherings. And for the immersive community, they saw an opportunity for immersive experiences to make their stand.

Though a pandemic accelerated progression, we were already isolated people. A lot of our entertainment comes from sitting at home, relaxing with friends while using the internet. Netflix is one of the biggest entertainment platforms in the world, providing content to millions of people. Amazon surged in popularity because anyone can buy anything, from computers to carpets, and have them delivered the next day. The same goes for grocery shopping, which is why Amazon bought Ring in 2018.[39] Video game companies let us play games with our friends from around the world – and is now a more significant industry than movies or music. Our habits have changed, and the biggest tech companies have given us the tools to expand our horizons from the comfort of our sofas. Yes, the current global pandemic forced people to stay at home and not go to restaurants, pubs, and cafes. Yet it also highlighted how much time we already spend at home, re-doing what we usually do on our laptops and TV.

The exception? Experiences. Both Millennials and Gen-Z want to spend their money on experiencing something new or exciting with friends, rather than owning products. According to research by Savvy, 73

[39] Gibbs, Samuel. 'Amazon Buys Video Doorbell Firm Ring for over $1bn.' The Guardian, 28 Feb. 2018. The Guardian,
https://www.theguardian.com/technology/2018/feb/28/amazon-buys-video-doorbell-ring-smart-home-delivery.

per cent prefer experiences over products in-store.[40] In response, London saw a massive surge in escape rooms, giving people memorable days and nights out. When people prize an impactful time with friends over the products they own, the streets of cities adapt.[41] But equally, VR and AR can offer impactful experiences as well, in much the same way that a powerful film can sway viewers. Why can't a powerful VR film be treated as an experience as well? That's where the market opportunity lies, long after the pandemic.

As we saw, the retail sector is adapting as fast as possible. Already beset by issues such as lower footfall, shifting consumer trends battered companies like House of Fraser and HMV. Over the last decade, companies shed thousands of jobs to keep their margins. The companies' roots were deep, but even they couldn't weather the flock of eCommerce companies that pecked away their profits.[42]

---

[40] '73% of Gen Z and Millennials Rate Experiences over Products.' Tamebay, 3 June 2019,
https://tamebay.com/2019/06/73-of-gen-z-and-millennials-rate-experiences-over-products.

[41] 'A New Role for Britain's High Streets.' The Economist, Mar. 2020. The Economist,
https://www.economist.com/britain/2020/03/05/a-new-role-for-britains-high-streets.

[42] Butler, Sarah. 'Great Britain's High Streets Lost More than 17,500 Chain Store Outlets in 2020.' The Guardian, 14 Mar. 2021. The Guardian,
https://www.theguardian.com/business/2021/mar/14/great-britain-high-streets-lost-more-than-17500-chain-stores-in-

The situation becomes worse when people cannot leave their house, or do not wish to. The solution is to bring all the retail experiences to the home. People go out to the shops to try on new clothes, instead of risking a purchase online. For online work, AR was a great fit, bringing an accurate try-before-you-buy tool. An example is Burberry, who incorporated AR features in their Google search results, as models that appear on flat surfaces.[43] Anyone can use Google for searching for products, so it makes sense to extend the capabilities towards virtual objects. When people search on Google, they have an 'intention,' and Google's algorithm is designed to try and match the search results to the user's intentions as closely as possible. If people search 'bread near me', Google responds with map markers of nearby bakeries and stores. If someone searches 'the best movies of 2019', Google will respond with a 'featured snippet' of movies, taken from a top-ranking article. Typically when people search for 'best handbags,' pieces come up from sites analysing the best ones. But surely the searcher would prefer to see more information on said handbags, straight from their mobile browser?

2020-covid.

[43] Stevens, Ben. 'Burberry Has Launched a New Google Search AR Feature for Its Products.' Latest Retail Technology News From Across The Globe - Charged, 25 Feb. 2020, https://www.chargedretail.co.uk/2020/02/25/burberry-has-launched-a-new-google-search-ar-feature-for-its-products/.

Why not see the best bags for yourself, on your table – would it satisfy your search enquiry?

Or take packaging. When people buy food, the packaging acts like an owned channel with an opportunity to massage their corporate messaging for their customers. Why not elevate the experience with AR? Why not take the customers along a brand journey, immerse them in the story, and draw data from their interactions that can be fed into other initiatives? As we mentioned earlier in the book, Coca-Cola is one example of a campaign in South Africa, prompting people to use face filters activated via their bottles. It is also why WebAR is critical for marketing; as many phones as possible should be able to activate the experience, regardless of the apps downloaded. If enabled via a simple in-browser link, then anyone can see the brand's marketing.

Now let's turn our attention to VR – and on the face of it, VR was perfect for a pandemic – with some supply-side issues. Covid-19 has drastically impacted the supply chain of Oculus, which are attempting to manufacture VR headsets as fast as possible. Buckled by the pandemic, Meta is working hard under drastically different conditions. 'Like other companies, we're experiencing some impact to our hardware production due to Covid-19,' a Meta spokesperson told Polygon in early 2020.[44]

---

[44] Kuchera, Ben. 'The Best VR Device Is Hard to Find, at the Worst Time.' Polygon, 13 Apr. 2020,

'We're taking precautions to ensure the safety of our employees, manufacturing partners and customers, and are monitoring the situation closely. We are working to restore availability as soon as we can.'

One repercussion was the rise of scalpers. Buying items in bulk, they sell the headsets on Amazon for a mark-up, reaping profit from the lack of supply. The people are the scum of the earth, but they indicate a clear economic principle; that when demand outstrips supply, prices rise. Locked inside with no way to travel or see friends, families are exploring new ways to dip into entertainment. Imagine being cramped in a small space, several feet in length and width, restricted and unable to venture far. Anyone would want a headset that breaks walls and let them venture further.

Similarly, video games are well-suited for the pandemic. Interactive experiences help people zone into another world in a fun and engaging way, communicating with friends via online features. *Animal Crossing: New Horizons*, where users can run their islands and visit others, released at a perfect time for those who can't travel. Even games like *Call of Duty: Warzone*, where people fight in a battle royale, nurture relationships via microphone chats.

And in VR? AltspaceVR has done incredibly well. Holding conferences and hosting groups, the platform became a meeting place for

https://www.polygon.com/2020/4/13/21218930/coronavirus -quarantine-oculus-quest-prices-sold-out-facebook-vr.

the immersive community. While Zoom calls may drain workers, and the endless phone calls with friends may become grating, meeting people in VR still has its pull.

Despite the boosted interest in VR, there are other factors in play. Take *Half-Life: Alyx*. Over a decade after the last *Half-Life* game, the next game in the franchise catapulted interest in VR headsets. As users scramble for headsets shortages followed the game's wake, impacting all VR headset manufacturers. *Half-Life: Alyx* was one of the biggest releases of 2020, spurring many to buy headsets. Gaming became the de facto use of VR beyond enterprise training. One estimation is that the game's release added one million VR users to Steam.[45]

Then there is the lack of hard numbers. Meta has been notably tight-lipped on the number of Oculus Quest units that have been sold. The same goes for HTC, Pico, and other VR headset manufacturers. With the restricted numbers, some speculate that the shortages are artificial; making slightly less than needed to encourage artificial demand, making the item more attractive. No evidence for this exists. Still, the Oculus Quest has been sold out multiple times over the last few months, long before the Covid-19 crisis. Yet while some factors led to its

---

[45] Lang, Ben. 'Analysis: 'Half-Life: Alyx' Adds Nearly 1 Million VR Users to Steam in Record Gain.' Road to VR, 2 May 2020, https://www.roadtovr.com/steam-survey-vr-headset-growth-april-2020-half-life-alyx/.

disappearance, new ones continue to ensure demand outstrips supply.

Social and video game experiences thrived – but not all areas saw the same growth. Notably, on-site VR marketing experiences took a major hit. Pre-pandemic, imagine walking past a train station, and you see an airline holding a stand with a couple of chairs and VR headsets. Users can then sit down, experience a new country, and decide whether they are interested in any deals related to the holiday. Simple but effective. The approach is also a popular way of using VR as a new thread of marketing in an integrated campaign. Yet in a time where people isolate, willingly or otherwise, how could these campaigns continue? The answer was they couldn't, and the tactic retreated to the shadows.

An alternative was VR experiences that can be downloaded for free and tried at home. REWIND (now part of Magnopus) created a short immersive experience for *Curfew: Join the Race*, as part of the Sky show's marketing campaign. Anyone can play it at home if they have the right headset, which in turn markets the show. The campaigns worked in theory, though numbers are difficult to find. The problem is discovery; how people see the experiences, to begin with. Even if advertised on social media, not everyone has a VR headset to try it out. And of everyone who has a VR headset, how many would be interested in the end-product? If the product's intended audience also happens to use VR headsets, then it could be useful.

In any case, there is not a clear link between marketing and VR during a pandemic. While VR arcades flourished in terms of entertainment before the pandemic, there are other ways to reach customers with a more definite link to KPIs. VR headsets are stuck as platforms, working better as experiences tried outside of the home.

Taking VR and AR together, it felt like mobile was imperative for immersive marketing for isolation. When people are stuck at home with their phones as entertainment, AR provides a deliverable way of guiding purchasing decisions. The content is more easily accessible than via a VR headset, outside of a closed system. Experiences can be shared via a web link, no matter what applications are installed. And there is a deliverable purpose, linked directly to the goals of the company with the data to prove it. When we are at home, we tend to browse our phones idly. With AR, brands can connect more intimately with their customers.

But beyond VR and AR, what about hybrid events? The hot word on everyone's tongues. Many believe that hybrid versions are an inevitability of the future of business – and immersive experiences have a role to play with it. There is still some debate on this; Microsoft said that working from home stifled productivity and creativity,[46] while a study says that half of the people want to continue working from home.[47]

Yet after the pandemic, we also hit a strange middle-place when it comes to hybrid events. As the world opens again, a lot of people – and particularly younger workers – want to head back to the office and speak face-to-face again.[48] Yet the corporate world is in a strange in-between where some people are coming back in, while others may be working from home. We'll see a hodgepodge of some calling in, others streaming via their kitchen counters, and perhaps another group strapped into VR headsets and using their hands. It's an experimental stage and one where businesses may build systems that will work across all parts of the office. Other surveys have shown a willingness to have options, and it comes down to productivity.[49] But in the end, businesses from

---

[46] 'Study of Microsoft Employees Shows How Remote Work Puts Productivity and Innovation at Risk.' GeekWire, 9 Sept. 2021, https://www.geekwire.com/2021/study-microsoft-employees-shows-remote-work-puts-productivity-innovation-risk/.

[47] 'Nearly Half of UK Professionals Want to Continue Remote Working, Study Reveals.' People Management, https://www.peoplemanagement.co.uk/news/articles/nearly-half-UK-professionals-continue-remote-working-study-reveals. Accessed 22 Jan. 2022.

[48] And who can blame them? The decaying array of pot plants that crowd cramped bedrooms aren't the best for conversations.

[49] 'Future of Corporate Events According to GBTA Research Study.' Hospitality Net, https://www.hospitalitynet.org/news/4104528.html. Accessed 22 Jan. 2022.

multiple different industries need to decide on what may work best for them.

Inevitably, there is no doubt that hybrid events and meetings are the most likely approach in the future. But the big money-maker question is, how many people will join virtual events or meetings in the future? The safe bet is that bigger events with a virtual component will be likely to draw in additional revenue. Both *Venice Film Festival* and *London Film Festival* happened again, and the accessibility of having virtual or VR elements only draws in more potential customers who can enjoy the festivities. Virtual events are an addition, not a replacement. For VR, I do not doubt that meetings for engineers to share multimedia files, such as CAD models of cars, will stick around.

The next question is whether customers will join virtual events in between all the parties, gatherings, and hugging[50] as restrictions lift and the world enters 2022 with some sense of normality. By charting the consumer patterns over the next few months, businesses can make appropriate plans for their expansion. In the end, this is why it feels like a strange time; the world is carefully watching how people shop and roam about, and making business plans based on their footfall. We're still in a transitory period between two types of normalcy, a tightrope precariously balancing between new revenue streams or business collapse. My money is on

---

[50] To put it politely.

the staying power of hybrid events and businesses maximising revenue with customers around the world instead of a country, and both VR and AR's new capabilities and applications sticking about. But in the end, it is a sociological question we are answering, and all we can do is keep an eye on the study numbers.

Key takeaways:
- The pandemic severely impacted how people consumed content.
- Companies both adapted to the changing conditions to the pandemic, as well as serviced the changing needs of the customers they serve.
- These trends will likely continue through 2022 as the world isolates itself further, for better and worse.

Charting the business direction of immersive technologies and the metaverse

Sometimes, the immersive industry feels like you're in the back of a car while the driver keeps saying 'we're almost there' for about ten years. The end is just around the corner, or over the next hill, or by the town ahead. But never is it here, now, in the present. Metaverse discussions are even worse, where you are unsure where the driver is even going.

The growth trajectory is seen as sluggish, lumbering up the growth curve at a leisurely pace while 5G and AI shoot upwards. Forecasts are always positive, and pine for a bold future that always seems to be beyond the horizon. Take the insights from CCS Insights as one example. As always, treat analyst stats and comments with a grain of salt; Meta hasn't given any hard numbers on the sales of their headsets, and some houses tend to fudge the definition of VR to make it seem bigger than it is.[51] All that being said, there is certainly evidence that the Quest 2 spiked interest in VR dramatically year-on-year, and the company forecasts that 70 million virtual and augmented reality devices will be sold in 2025, with a market value of $2bn.[52]

---

[51] One time, a company (not CCS Insight) labelled VR to be the same as mobile VR, then said that VR penetration was massive as people had smartphones. Cripes.

[52] 'Things Are Finally Going Well for Extended Reality.'

The large market share will be reflective of both consumer and enterprise applications, which will likely contribute far more than $21bn by the time we reach 2030 and the technology gets exponentially adopted across more countries.

A separate report said that there was an increased appetite for XR investments after the pandemic, with AR enterprise and XR infrastructure remaining the most interesting areas for investors.[53] A surge in spending is certainly keeping companies buoyed through the pandemic, and the general sentiment is that the new technologies will help workers collaborate better and help develop new skills in the workforce. But how many companies will survive the pandemic - or perhaps should? As government support recedes over time, several 'zombie' companies that should have failed will likely collapse. Some of these will likely be VR / AR companies, though it is difficult to say which ones. Many metaverse start-ups would also be bloated by hype, rather than grounded with reasonable goals; once the balloon pops, many would shutter.

Still, many companies have a high level of trust in the future of immersive – perhaps a few

CCS Insight, 2 July 2021, https://www.ccsinsight.com/blog/things-are-finally-going-well-for-extended-reality/.

[53] *Immerse UK → UK Immersive Tech: VC Investment Report.* https://www.immerseuk.org/resources/uk-immersive-tech-vc-investment-report/. Accessed 22 Jan. 2022.

more than Qualcomm, supplying the silicon that powers many, many immersive headsets. Qualcomm is very excited about the future of immersive technologies. 'Over the next few years, it's going to grow exponentially,' said Qualcomm VP and GM of XR Hugo Swart. 'Every person on the planet is likely going to have one.'[54] He highlights the four parallel tracks of immersive technologies, including VR headsets, enterprise headsets (HoloLens), smart glasses, and wireless viewers. And eventually, a number of these could converge into a true AR device—though the actual specifications and details are several years into the future.

Following chip manufacturers like Qualcomm is important to keep tabs on a component of building future hardware. Their recent work with 5G mmWave technologies is an example of how it can branch out into XR, for example.[55]

Bear in mind that optimism is incredibly high as well, particularly in the venture capital space. Many immersive companies are suddenly getting a lot of money to finance their growth, with a renewed interest in expanding their

---

[54] Roettgers, Janko. 'The Big Story.' Protocol — The People, Power and Politics of Tech, 24 June 2021, https://www.protocol.com/newsletters/next-up/paths-to-consumer-ar?rebelltitem=1#rebelltitem1?rebelltitem=1.

[55] Condon, Stephanie. 'Qualcomm Demos the Latest in 5G MmWave Technologies.' ZDNet, https://www.zdnet.com/article/qualcomm-demos-the-latest-in-5g-mmwave-technologies/. Accessed 22 Jan. 2022.

operations or speeding up their growth. Here are a few examples from early 2021, all in a single week:

- JigSpace raised $4.7m in Series A funding;[56]
- Tripp raised $11m in Series A funding;[57]
- Virti raised $10m in Series A funding;[58]
- VRChat raised $80m in Series D funding;[59]
- Magnopus acquired REWIND.[60]

---

[56] 'Apple and Snap Partner JigSpace, the 'Canva for 3D,' Raises a $4.7M Series A.' TechCrunch, https://social.techcrunch.com/2021/06/30/apple-and-snap-partner-jigspace-the-canva-for-3d-raises-a-4-7m-series-a/. Accessed 22 Jan. 2022.

[57] 'Psychedelic VR Meditation Startup Tripp Raises $11 Million Series A.' TechCrunch, https://social.techcrunch.com/2021/06/24/psychedelic-vr-meditation-startup-tripp-raises-11-million-series-a/. Accessed 22 Jan. 2022.

[58] 'Training Platform Virti Raises $10M Series A Led by IQ Capital to Teach Soft Skills in VR.' TechCrunch, https://social.techcrunch.com/2021/06/29/training-platform-virti-raises-10m-series-a-led-by-iq-capital-to-teach-soft-skills-in-vr/. Accessed 22 Jan. 2022.

[59] Hayden, Scott. "VRChat' Secures $80M Series D Funding to Create Its Own Digital Economy.' Road to VR, 28 June 2021, https://www.roadtovr.com/vrchat-80m-series-d-funding/.

[60] 'Mission:ISS' Magnopus Acquires XR Design Studio REWIND.' GMW3, https://www.gmw3.com/2021/07/missioniss-magnopus-acquires-xr-design-studio-rewind/. Accessed 22 Jan. 2022.

Why is everyone raising cash now? The Gartner fans would say we have climbed our way out of the trough of disillusionment and scaling up the slope of enlightenment.[61] We may even reach the plateau of productivity, though we'll have a few casualties along the way. But the point is that there is a renewed trust in immersive technologies, and their impact across social worlds, meditation, and 3D model creation. The trend was accelerated by the metaverse, as a wave of VCs funded companies built the potential infrastructure for it. For me, this is one of the safest areas to follow when it comes to the metaverse; follow where the money flows towards building the foundations, rather than a company building a social service on top of it.

The way I am wording this implies that the growth will be equally distributed across AR and VR, as the immersive space grows together. Not so. The most likely area of healthy growth will remain in enterprise-side applications until the consumer-end hardware and software get good enough. But for now, we are seeing the bricks of the future laid down.

The best we can take away from it is that investors have a renewed hope on the underlying principles of immersive. The investments will either pay off, or crash a la the 2017-style bubble. Personally, I hope that we

[61] 'Gartner Hype Cycle Research Methodology.' Gartner, https://www.gartner.com/en/research/methodologies/gartner-hype-cycle. Accessed 22 Jan. 2022.

celebrate with bubbles of champagne over financial pops.

Holistically, we are seeing steady growth in the area; it is just not as quick as some people may want. And the more stories that come out where the Quest 2 is pushing the market forward, the more it becomes clear that we need more competitors. While it is great that Meta is investing so much into the market until it becomes self-sustaining, it would be great to see more consumer-end hardware that innovates a little more. We may have some similarities with this after TikTok's acquisition of Pico, but we'll have to see where the overall strategy will go.[62]

What we can all agree on is that the trajectory is upwards, but it is not hitting the exponential growth that many companies may want. The trouble with exponential growth, however, is that it always looks like small numbers until it explodes in popularity.

This leads naturally to enterprise training – which will always be strong, and companies will either swell in to provide services, or pivot towards the honeypot. On 22 April 2020, Magic Leap announced that they were laying off employees to cope with the Covid-19 crisis.[63] The official

[62] Robertson, Adi. 'TikTok's Parent Company Acquires VR Headset Maker Pico.' The Verge, 30 Aug. 2021, https://www.theverge.com/2021/8/30/22648282/bytedance -tiktok-vr-pico-hardware.

[63] 'Charting a new course.' Magicleap.com.

blog did not give any specific numbers, but Bloomberg reported that it was about 1000; the layoffs coincide with a change of course, away from its consumer ventures towards enterprise matters.[64]

Like many other businesses, Covid-19 drastically impacted Magic Leap and forced its hand with its decisions. But these decisions were coming anyway. Magic Leap was going through some troubled times, and changes were likely coming down the line. While Covid-19 was the straw that broke the camel's back, the camel was already carrying a lot of capital (and emotional) baggage.

The blog made clear their aims: 'The recent changes to the economic environment have decreased availability of capital and the appetite for longer-term investments. While our leadership team, board, and investors still believe in the long-term potential of our IP, the near-term revenue opportunities are currently concentrated on the enterprise side.' The transition makes sense. When following the money, enterprise-related activities are a winner. Sources I've spoken to that have partnered with Magic Leap informed me that, in many cases, the partnerships were more for PR than money.

https://www.magicleap.com/news/news/charting-a-new-course. Accessed 22 Jan. 2022.

[64] 'Magic Leap Cuts Half of Jobs.' Bloomberg.com. https://www.bloomberg.com/news/articles/2020-04-22/magic-leap-is-said-to-cut-half-of-jobs-in-major-restructuring?sref=gni836kR. Accessed 22 Jan. 2022.

The best way of thinking about these projects was the dazzle and point-of-concept showpieces, rather than generating a large lump of cash. Such approaches could lead to more money down the line, but in the short-term, it's best to treat the approach as an investment for the future.

Consider the change of direction and its ramifications for the wider industry. Magic Leap is one of the most hyped companies in the tech world. After years of secrecy, the product launched its first headset to great applause. Yet after the release, years of further secrecy followed, not fully unveiling their numbers as reports trickled through. I still remember fondly watching Dinosaur's prowl through a room as David Attenborough narrated their details. I also wish them all the best for their pivot towards enterprise activities. But based on the volume of reports over the years, COVID-19 didn't cause Magic Leap's change in course. It was the weight of its decisions over several years, long before the pandemic.

These macro trends explain why HTC, Meta, and Microsoft all supply enterprise variations of their immersive offerings, with expansive teams that service the needs of their clients – few more profitably than the military.

The militarisation of commercial products is both exciting and nerve-wracking, with Microsoft working particularly closely with the US Army.[65] Their innovative approach is striking;

Microsoft engineers and army personnel are working together to build and develop the product, so it is fit for purpose when deployed. As the article noted, 'The tech giant's engineers are in the field with soldiers, listening to their criticisms and suggestions, and sometimes rewriting software on the spot. 'It's cold, it's raining, and you see these young people from Microsoft … they're out there at 2:00 in the morning. They got their headphones on, they're under their blankets with their hoodie, and they're coding,' Potts said. 'They're having an absolute blast."[66]

Then, having worked together several years ago with a smaller contract, the U.S. Army announced that their entire Close Combat Force will be outfitted with HoloLens devices.[67] Think of it as commanders feeding information to soldiers while they are deployed on the field. While the three Bethesdas[68] worth of cash grabbed

---

[65] Gill, Jaspreet. 'DoD 'Agile' Software Development Still Too Slow: GAO.' Breaking Defense, 12 June 2020, https://breakingdefense.sites.breakingmedia.com/2020/06/dod-agile-software-development-still-too-slow-gao/.

[66] Did you know it's not called the HoloLens on the filed? It's renamed the Integrated Visual Augmentation System. Catchy name, if it's ever sold in a shop.

[67] 'Microsoft $22bn US Army Deal for Hololens Moves Forward.' Bloomberg.com. https://www.bloomberg.com/news/articles/2021-03-31/microsoft-22-billion-u-s-army-deal-for-hololens-moves-forward. Accessed 22 Jan. 2022.

[68] Microsoft bought Bethesda for a few billion dollars, as part of their strategy with Xbox.

headlines, the deal also showed a high level of trust. The agreement will last for five years, with a possibility to extend another five. The deal also includes some Azure cloud services; remember that Azure is a core revenue driver for the company, so we may see more immersive-related content as part of it in the future as it integrates further with Microsoft's cloud services.

It's highly probable that its interconnected web of services and hardware–HoloLens, Azure, expertise–helped it win the contract, compared to other competitors who might only fill one area sufficiently. It's also why companies like Microsoft are so important to follow within the immersive space. While Apple is a hardware company attempting to diversify towards services, and VR / AR-specific platforms provide the tools of creation, it's the synthesis of all parts that puts Microsoft in a strong position.

Not everyone is comfortable with military applications of emerging technologies–see any history book. But history has also shown us that military or government investment accelerates research and work into the area, identifying new ways in which it could seep down into society as well.

Overall, the business direction will continue to double down on the enterprise side, while social apps will develop slowly but steadily. I see no point in postulating whether Apple's arrival on the scene will change anything; no product has been seen yet, and their strategy isn't clear. But what is evident is that there is a slow and gradual adoption with enterprises which is picking up steam, leading to a shortage of specialised labour to handle the increased activities.

Linked to this is the growth of reality-based platforms. I'm seeing a new trend where the new product announcements are moving from constructed virtual worlds, to importing real-life locations. It is less about sitting in a meeting room designed for virtual conferencing, and more about sitting in a piazza in Rome while talking over work matters. There are pros and cons to both; I personally would much rather sit in a café and talk shop, but it's certainly more distracting to work in. But the concept has wide applications across collaboration, property, and retail verticals.

A great example of this is Varjo's Reality Cloud. Headset users can scan their environment, then transport other users virtually into the same space. Cool, though expensive, too; it currently only works with their XR-3 headset, which sells for over $5,000. But in concept, it's a wonderful way for users to import scans of their own homes or areas and share them with their (incredibly affluent) friends. For businesses, it provides an incredibly immersive way to show a property and its details, live and with other collaborators.

All of this links to Varjo's vision of the metaverse. I say their vision, because nearly every single company has their version of the concept with no consensus on what it means. But Varjo wants to introduce one which is grounded, creating a twin of reality that people can take a look at. But overall, I like this vision, and there is a place for it. I wouldn't call it a metaverse necessarily; more a helpful tool for businesses to use, to help collaborate better or share spaces more clearly. It won't be a lived-in reality, just a useful way to convey information.

I found the platforms and metaverse argument all the time across my work, where they want to 'own' the space where people conduct their lives. The argument makes sense; by owning the ground where business works, you have a more stable and lucrative growth trajectory. McDonalds is a real-estate business rather than a hamburger shop, doubling down on the land where the burgers are cooked.[69] Take the same concept and put it on the virtual level, and you have a recipe for success.

Creating an expansive office is certainly the view of Meta as well. In an interview between Andrew Bosworth and John Carmack, they suggest that headsets could become fully functional personal computers. Think of it as typing up all your work via hand tracking, browsing the web, and collaborating all in one virtual world – all in one 'infinite office.' The key goal is to get the software up to scratch, and innovate on the

---

[69] If you have a free evening, *The Founder* is a great story on the origins of McDonalds. Wonderful acting performance by Michael Keaton.

hardware over time so the experience gets better and better.[70]

My first initial thought after reading the transcription was, computers are good enough. Most office workers will choose a handy laptop over a VR headset that lacks the app libraries for work. The depth and complexity of the laptop's system dwarf VR headsets, and choosing one over the other feels like picking a DVD player over the internet. Typically with markets, they address a pain point or business need; laptops serve the role incredibly well, and VR needs to do things they couldn't do otherwise to succeed.

Having said that, another part of me sees a future where they are deployed across very particular businesses, but it won't be widespread. One example includes enterprise companies that require close collaboration, but the commute times are too long or the living accommodations are quite cramped. Deploying a fleet of headsets to a remote-working workforce makes sense, at least in those times. Meta is following the money on this; the digital workplace money is estimated to be worth $72bn by 2026. But to choose a VR headset over, say, a cheap laptop, is unlikely for most companies.[71]

---

[70] *John Carmack & Andrew Bosworth Twitter Spaces Recording.* 23 Apr. 2021, https://uploadvr.com/carmack-bosworth-recording-twitter/.

[71] *Digital Workplace Market Worth $72.2 Billion by 2026 - Exclusive Report by MarketsandMarkets.* https://finance.yahoo.com/news/digital-workplace-market-

HTC are on the same boat, supplying a range of products to work with businesses. The company released the VIVE Sync (which I tried out), a collaboration platform entering free Beta. It's not every day that I interview someone in virtual reality; but still, the company kindly invited me to speak to Graham Wheeler, General Manager EMEA at the company in the immersive arena. I left it thinking that VIVE Sync offers a compelling package. AltspaceVR and ENGAGE both provide similar services, with community options built into both platforms. HTC's version offers something different; one dedicated for companies working remotely across the world, with tools that service businesses rather than hobbies. I feel that my experiences are helpful for collaborative work, so here are my full experiences.

I quickly made an avatar before the interview. The platform offers a range of options for hair, suits, shirts, colour, and height (standing and sitting). After going through the options, I've found that it was diverse enough for most people. The diversity of options lets me express myself adequately, though it doesn't reach *VRChat* levels of customisability. Then again, I am unsure how many workers would want their avatars to be anime characters or miniatures riding tanks.

Entering a room was slick. Users can either type a small number or scan a QR code to fill the form automatically. The headset could be

worth-72-150000731.html. Accessed 22 Jan. 2022.

used on a computer, so it makes sense that it presents an option to use AR codes while people are already sitting down, making the process as seamless as possible. It's a neat feature that I hope more companies use.

Once filled, I popped into a new room. I beamed into an open area, a city on the horizon and a simple circle in the middle. 'Hello!' Mr Wheeler called, waving at me. 'Hello,' I responded, looking at my hands. I had elbows; not remarkable for most people, but interesting for other VR users.

That sense of immersion followed us to a table too. I felt myself following the same habits that I do in a regular meeting; not quite making eye contact, making notes on the table, and looking around the room absentmindedly. My common ticks followed me in virtual reality. I recalled speaking to a few researchers about how much of our body we use when having a conversation. Not just our words, but our eyes, hands, and general bearing. All of these transferred to VIVE Sync, as we waved our hands to emphasise points. Some other perks include ruffling virtual hair, or shaking hands while ending a meeting.

Not all of it is perfect. A part of me wished I could teleport files onto the table, which people could read as they watch the giant screen. I was able to read files from a tablet but wished I could read on a table as well.

It was not lost on me that it was released during a pandemic, and I asked if it impacted developments across the industry? 'No, actually,' Mr Wheeler responded. 'We've found that the situation has accelerated the need for collaboration tools, and while using the tools they work effectively as a team.'

Is there a business case? I can see it. Virtual meetings offer a sense of space that eases participants, with a more natural feel to how a session should go. Nothing will beat meeting in person, but VIVE Sync is still a step above Zoom, or the impersonal nature of Slack.

HTC also thinks it is the future of collaboration. 'Unlike any other tool or medium, VR can connect and engage remote teams and employees as if they were together in the same physical room,' said David Sapienza, AVP Content Development & Production, HTC VIVE. 'Vive Sync enables colleagues and partners across the world to interact in a shared virtual space, increasing productivity, collaboration and team chemistry. The future of work is rapidly becoming more global and more remote and VR is the solution needed to succeed in this new reality.'

Is he right? Time will tell. But initial impressions are very positive. We will see more and more competitors enter the market, and walled gardens are rising around the VR ecosystem. Ultimately, I see a future where companies work within remote virtual worlds, hopping from virtual place to place as they make plans and execute campaigns. But while some will be hopping around the virtual micro-metaverse, most will be content hopping onto Teams calls while checking their Twitter.

Of all the areas that can be lucrative in the short term, few are as promising as exercise. During the pandemic, VR saw a sizable boom in activity, and one of the most popular activities (alongside gaming) is exercise. Restricted in their homes and perhaps wanting to do something different, users don the headset and release the pressure with some jabs and squats. The demand is there; CCS Insight released a survey stating that the 'majority' of VR users work out at least once a week.[72]

The discussion links to the profitability of subscription services, too. Following the heels of Viveport, Meta added the capabilities in 2021. Adding the capabilities makes sense; if done correctly, subscription-based services are incredibly lucrative for companies who want a consistent cash flow and tight relationship with their customers. Apple's transition towards providing more services is one example, as well as Microsoft's successful push of business-related applications.

Companies are responding quickly. I spoke to FitXR CEO Sam Cole, who is incorporating a subscription model into his fitness VR company. For $9.99 a month, users

---

[72] 'Virtual Reality Gets a Boost during the Pandemic.' CCS Insight, https://www.ccsinsight.com/press/company-news/virtual-reality-gets-a-boost-during-the-pandemic/. Accessed 22 Jan. 2022.

can receive a new class every day of the week which they can hop into to sweat it out. (This compares favourably to Supernatural, which is $20 a month). This comes along with a whole host of new additions such as multiplayer and a new HIIT studio, but what struck me as the most interesting is the transition itself. 'Oculus launching subscriptions represents a coming of age moment for VR,' he said, 'as developers can provide significantly more value to their customers.' For FitXR, it's a bold pivot that is in line with their long-term growth goals.

I don't personally exercise much in VR. At best I get sweaty after playing more active games for some time, as I personally prefer running. But the burgeoning demand shows that people are willing to wear headsets to get fit, and a subscription model is a great way to deliver consistent content and a broad swathe of services for their users. Not all verticals would suit a sub-model – but fitness is bang on target.

Key takeaways:
- Financial investment exploded in 2021, as companies tap into the potential of immersive technologies.
- Prioritise following companies providing the infrastructure of the metaverse, rather than the services that would be built on top of it.
- While I am cynical about business-related applications, continued innovations could

match the needs of workers and help elevate their productivity over time.

- Enterprise training will remain strong as a sector, for years to come.
- Fitness is one of the most lucrative areas of immersive, and worth closely following.

AR glasses: Hype and realism

The conversation around AR glasses is both aggravating and exciting. Aggravating because people espouse the potential of AR glasses, and how it will be the next computing platform with a similar staying power as the mobile phone – even though they have never tried them. And exciting because, well, they might be right.

We're at the preliminary stage where technology companies are doubling down on AR glasses development, building the future behind lab doors, and resolving an incredibly difficult technical challenge. The glasses need to be light, attractive, and have enough computing power to make the high spec bump worth it. All while handing the heat of running metallic components on people's heads.

Many thinkers see the arrival of AR glasses as the start of a new era of a paradigm shift, where people can interact with a virtual overlay of the real world and paint a new canvas of information. Imagine attending a tourist site and seeing AR images and information about the location itself. The same technology can also be used as a tool of terror; imagine the same site being splayed by virtual slurs and graffiti that ravage the same location, unseen by unspecced eyes. Directions lead people down the right streets, a guiding hand through the maze of roads and paths. Messages and emails filter through the headset, nudging users with gentle tugs of information to read then or later.

say. As Snap is not disclosing the amount, then my fingers are crossed that it'll be enough to pay itself back over the next few years.

AR can also be used for more bombastic purposes, such as the world's first AR smartphone launch.[79] Did the OnePlus Nord benefit from a unique unveiling? Or did the experience crumble under its finicky frame? The result is a mix of both.

The cons started at the beginning. It initially showed several 2D videos in the beginning to outline the presentation. Normally this is fine... except in AR, when the video is tiny and the subtitles even smaller. Showing a narrow frame of a video within a smartphone, while holding it up to watch it all, is not fun. Who wants to see a video within a video?

But the pros came after. Seeing a model of the phone where I can look all around it, and see all the specs detailed out, is fantastic. A live stream or video doesn't compare to the product visualisation of a model in front of you. 150,000 people viewing a realistic model of a new phone, all at once. That's an amazing benefit and achievement.

AR launches can work, so long as it cuts to the chase. Anything else is fiddly and sucks any fun from the hype of a global unveiling.

---

[79] McCann, John. 'OnePlus Nord Launch Date Confirmed and It'll Be a World's First - Here's How to Watch.' TechRadar, 7 July 2020,
https://www.techradar.com/news/oneplus-nord-launch-date.

When doing new things, it's okay to gut the traditional steps – a video introduction, for example – to help the person understand a product.

So we have a playing field where AR has a powerful effect on shoppers. Digital advertising is still incredibly effective, which is why it sucks up a good chunk of the marketing budget each year.[80] Though smaller and more focused, these immersive experiences have a tangible and powerful impact on shoppers. If AR glasses reach a high penetration rate, these AR activities will become more important. The field is there – now we need the glasses themselves.

Now we have an understanding of how AR can be used, let's dip into the hardware. I've mentioned before that the challenge is immense – though arguably more important than software. As Alan Kay once said, 'People who are serious about software should make their hardware.'[81] Heavy and clunky challenges that look strange will never sell as well as the cheap but stylish frames that local pharmacies sell. Building the necessary components takes a lot of brainpower

---

[80] Gray, Alistair. 'Consumer Brands to Protect Ad Budgets Even as Other Costs Spiral.' Financial Times, 22 Aug. 2021, https://www.ft.com/content/6367b03e-76e9-4369-bf3b-786b470d84ed.

[81] *Steve Jobs Quoted Alan Kay with 'People Who Are Really Serious about Software Sh... | Hacker News.* https://news.ycombinator.com/item?id=2763367. Accessed 22 Jan. 2022.

– and in response, many tech companies are making strategic acquisitions to strengthen their technical prowess.

For instance, Meta hit a deal with Plessey to supply AR displays. In 2020, Meta 'struck a deal to buy all the augmented reality displays made by... Plessey, as the social network looks to build AR glasses capable of overlaying virtual objects onto the real world.'[82] This is not an acquisition, which would have brought regulatory scrutiny; it is a supply-side exclusive deal, which speeds up the process while owning a part of the chain.

This is an acquisition of ownership. Some headset and glasses manufacturers prefer to control the entire design process and make all the components, such as Vuzix. Other companies prefer to have partnerships with some manufacturers to help build an overall product. There are pros and cons to both approaches, with a company like Meta can bankroll an entire industry, it's a sound business decision.

Then take Snap, who are making frames of their own and bought their own companies, such as WaveOptics – who create waveguides – for a cool ~$500m.[83] The waveguides bend the

[82] 'Facebook Strikes Deal for AR Displays, Squeezing Out Apple.' The Information,
https://www.theinformation.com/articles/facebook-strikes-deal-for-ar-displays-trying-to-squeeze-out-apple. Accessed 22 Jan. 2022.

[83] Heath, Alex. 'Snap Is Buying Its AR Display Supplier for

light in such a way as to create crisp images, and the technology is, for lack of a better word, astonishing. In February 2020 I met the team as they unveiled their Katana version, which was awesome to see.[84] Their Oxford offices showcased their technology, and I was wowed by the sophistication of what goes behind their waveguides (and my brain was slightly fried as well).

Such moves also link back to the printing of lenses, attempting to make it as seamless as possible. Luxexcel addressed this, and launched a platform that helps companies 3D print AR prescription lenses. The benefit is that a manufacturing process that can create and send prescription lenses means it can service people who need the glasses. People like me, where I am as blind as a bat.

The significance of this is that a lot of people would benefit as most need prescription lenses. 'To compete in the race to launch consumer-ready smart glasses, eyewear manufacturers need to address prescription in their smart glasses devices,' said Fabio Esposito, Chief Executive Officer at Luxexcel. 'More than 75 per cent of the adult world

More than $500 Million.' The Verge, 21 May 2021, https://www.theverge.com/2021/5/21/22447150/snap-waveoptics-acquisition-500m-spectacles-waveguides.

[84] 'Enabling AR Glasses: How WaveOpics Supplies the Key Components.' Immersive Wire, 3 Feb. 2020, https://www.immersivewire.com/waveoptics-ar-glasses-katana/.

population today requires prescription lenses. Luxexcel provides a disruptive solution where smart technology is seamlessly combined with a prescription lens, rather than adding prescription power to the smart device as an afterthought.'[85] The technology is based on VisionPlatform 7, which is designed to print lenses for commercial glasses. It also has some flexibility, letting designers make the glasses they want.

It's another part of the landscape where companies need a quick and easy way to shoot lenses to consumers, and Luxexcel is providing the platform that makes it easier to execute. I am curious to see how effective it is, and whether it can work on a massive scale. If it does, then that's one part of the supply chain done and dusted.

We're going to see more companies battle it out on the component side in the future, as they harness the technology and brainpower to deploy innovative specs. Snap's version is more of an enthusiast developer edition, a 30-minute-of-battery toy for people to play around with. Acquisitions like WaveOptics are vital to solidifying their position, now and into the future.

Additionally, hardware forms the bedrock of work, but overlayed on top is the software that runs it all. While the OS is difficult to talk about at this early stage, an important factor to consider

---

[85] 'Launch of Manufacturing Platform of Smartglasses Lenses.' Luxexcel, 14 July 2021, https://www.luxexcel.com/luxexcel-launches-platform-for-manufacturing-of-prescription-lenses-for-smartglasses/.

is mapping technologies. Reading the environment to place virtual objects is important, but so is being able to read the world around the glasses, and paint a map of how they connect with one another.

Take another one of Niantic's acquisitions, such as 6D.ai; a company developing tech that can rapidly scan the 3D environment around them.[86] Super useful if you want a Bulbasaur to jump on your sleeping roommate, sure, but it also allows them to build out more sophisticated uses of the technology. While Niantic rolled back on outdoor activities for pandemic reasons, the long-term trajectory is clear; Niantic wants to maintain its lucrative partnerships and provide immersive mobile experiences. Remember, Niantic is also creating AR glasses of their own; the team wants to pioneer in software as well as hardware in the years to come.[87]

Such hardware updates are also linked to the progression of input methods as well; the more seamless the interactions, the more likely that people will use them. Consider how Meta

---

[86] 'Niantic Squares up against Apple and Facebook with Acquisition of AR Startup 6D.Ai.' TechCrunch, https://social.techcrunch.com/2020/03/31/niantic-acquires-ar-startup-6d-ai-as-the-game-creator-squares-up-against-apple-facebook/. Accessed 22 Jan. 2022.

[87] 'Niantic CEO Shares Teaser Image of AR Glasses Device.' TechCrunch, https://social.techcrunch.com/2021/03/29/niantic-ceo-shares-teaser-image-of-ar-glasses-device/. Accessed 22 Jan. 2022

unveiled some of its work on new hand gestures for both VR and AR devices, and it's got my brain whirring.[88] Some benefits of the work include:

- **Accessibility for impaired people:** As one example, a person born without a hand can control a virtual version because the wrist device tracks neural signals. The ramifications are immense, opening the doors for more people to access their tech; it is only a good thing, from my perspective.
- **Fast interactions:** While typical hand tracking requires good cameras and lighting, with a slight lag, neural interactions can cut the delay. It is worth noting that the same benefits can come with haptic gloves as well.
- **Better interactions for AR glasses:** No-one wants to wave their hands in front of their face while travelling or commuting. Having a wrist device works simply with a future version of the specs.

---

[88] 'Inside Facebook Reality Labs: Wrist-Based Interaction for the next Computing Platform.' Facebook Technology, 18 Mar. 2021, https://tech.fb.com/inside-facebook-reality-labs-wrist-based-interaction-for-the-next-computing-platform/.

Tracking neural signals prompts privacy concerns, which Neuromotor Interfaces Director Thomas Reardon comments on: 'Neural data like this is quite personal and we treat this issue as part of our research set. The problem of how to deal with information that is this personal and engage in a way that is pro-human and on behalf of users. I will tell you that we are deeply committed to transparency as scientists, to engaging in the world of publishing and the world of public engagement, so that we can explain to people why we use this data, how we use it, and what kinds of user experiences are enabled by it.'[89]

All of this is a long way from public release, but it's interesting to see the company engineer its vision of spatial computing across multiple different approaches. It also reinforces my belief in the most important component of immersive devices: the control method. It acts as a gateway to all experiences, as a finicky substitute would ward interested users away. But get it right, and you have a new interaction device on the same level as the computer mouse for PCs.

We've mentioned Google before, and their approach can be summarised as a shrug followed by a skitter-scatter of announcements here and there. But their influence is massive; there have been 200 million AR-related

---

[89] *Facebook Research On Wrist-Based Hand Tracking & Haptics*. 18 Mar. 2021, https://uploadvr.com/facebook-wrist-based-hand-tracking-haptics/.

searches on the platform since it was launched, and they showed off some athletes in AR as well. Additionally, Live View AR had been updated on Google Maps to provide street labels, landmarks, and indoor directions in places like airports and malls. A blessing, considering how many families get lost in transit hubs.[90]

This doubles down to their strength, as Google has a massive advantage with their mapping tools. By building on their already-established dominance in the mapping space, adding contextual information with immersive tech is a natural step to maintain their lead. But rather than deliver new services which help users, the company is content with building out their core features by helping them more and more.

In short, the development of AR glasses is secretive, yet it can lead to a major impact across the world. We're in the hypothetical stage where we meander across the halls of potential, but with very little guidance on what the specs can do. But despite this, I am incredibly excited about it. I like the idea of another world on top of the real, where I can have my virtual stamp and play unique titles. Let's keep track of where it goes, and see if my excitement is validated in the long term.

---

[90] *The Immersive Wire - 19 May 2021 (News Edition).* https://us15.campaign-archive.com/?u=79a59169e0b77435ae7265651&id=c958efa7b7. Accessed 22 Jan. 2022.

Key takeaways:
- The potential of AR shopping is there, as it powerfully engages people.
- Companies are focusing on the development of components for AR glasses, and will be a key differentiator as they continue their growth.
- It is hard to know what AR glasses will look like in the future, but they have major development hurdles to circumvent.
- Though it is hard to tell if consumers want them, it is an exciting area to follow closely.

Alternative uses of immersive technologies

Readers, it is time to go niche. The following areas are not as covered in mainstream news or media, but I feel represents some of the most important developments when it comes to immersive technologies.[91] The chapter will cover areas that show some promise, such as spatial audio, and others which I am cynical about, such as teaching schoolchildren. Across all of these, I hope you find the insights useful.

First, let's touch on spatial audio. Strip away graphics and gestures, and audio is one of the most important parts of any experience. Good graphics go far, and mechanics make a world feel alive – but good audio is necessary. No audio is like a house without walls. Spatial audio is not as sexy as good graphics, but its impact far exceeds pixel counts.

Spatial audio is a step up from regular audio. Typically, audio has very simplistic

---

[91] Perhaps the most niche I have come across is a memorial service in VR; I was particularly touched by the VR memorial held for Christian Long. The pandemic hampered all parts of life, from the general food shop to attending funerals. All distances feel longer when stuck at home, and longer still when a friend and colleague has passed on. In response, Steve Bambury, Chris Madsen, and Mike Armstrong held a service in Engage. VR memorials have perks, too. Not everyone can have planes fly over, for example. But at times like these, when the most basic of services cannot be attended, there was a poignancy to it.

surround-sound qualities, such as left and right. The biggest stretches they can do is whether an instrument is playing to the left or right of an individual. Spatial audio takes the next step and lets musicians and developers simulate sounds above and behind people as well. An example may be playing a gunshot behind someone, or a plane flying above someone.

We've already seen some incredible work in the area. Oliver Kadel runs a great podcast on audio and immersive projects, interviewing key figures bringing their work to life. Perhaps my favourite is by Playlines and Harry Shotta, called *Consequences;* an immersive AR rap experience that's a part-concept album, part-silent disco, and part-close encounter with the British grime scene. Yes, you read that correctly. It's a real mix, but Muki Kulhan did a fantastic job. But what helped it turn up a notch was the Bose AR glasses, which track when people are near a certain location to continue the story. Location-based storytelling, enabled with spatial audio.

Having glasses with spatial audio means that people can hear voices around them, almost like a ghost, and check out audio queues based on what's said. The potential for immersive tech is immense. The discussion bleeds into VR as well. HMDs help to bring people into new worlds, immersing people with swords, shields, or guns as they walk through a new location. High-end audio is the cherry on top of the cake, tying the great graphics and gameplay together like glue.

By comparison, poor audio cripples a good virtual reality game. Imagine wandering around the world and you hear rusty birds cawing in the distance, or an audio file that plays slightly too late when a sword swipes in front of you. Audio is as much part of the virtual world as the plans and the animals, and must never be sacrificed for the sake of an experience.

That said, mobile devices are not the best way of viewing films. Nothing beats sitting back in a comfortable chair among friends, and watching the latest blockbuster on a massive screen among friends and family. But for those who are at home, the innovation is enough to spark some amazing work. The same principles apply to VR films and games, too. The same principles apply to VR films as well. Imagine looking at an immersive film from *Raindance Immersive*, with conversations happening all around a person. Having voices above and behind individuals contributes to the immersion of artistic pieces, hopefully driving some innovative items in the future.

Imagine solving a murder mystery in VR, roaming around a room in Quest 2 headset searching for clues. Then you hear a pitter-patter behind you, and you look behind to see mice crawling across the room. Or perhaps while playing a VR shooter, and you hear gunshots above you; a sniper aiming at you. VR improves immersion, but spatial audio finishes the package.

Alongside spatial audio, we have immersive technologies and children's education as well. My perspective hasn't shifted over the last few years; schools and teachers have more important aspects to focus on than the high-end power that VR can bring. In the UK we have underpaid teachers who work long hours, and some schools struggle to even service their teaching supplies. No matter the power of VR, I still think funds should flow towards other vital areas right now.

That said, I do not doubt that immersive technologies will continue to impact education. AR apps can be used with a variety of smartphones that children own, and the impact that VR has is extraordinary. Barriers of access are lowering, and more people can use education apps. However, during Covid-19, select companies said that VR and AR will help everyone have lost touch with reality. Education is struggling, and remote learning solutions cannot match the power of classrooms during this time. While beneficial, it won't help everyone during the crisis.

To be clear, I fully recognise the benefits of immersive technologies and education. Multiple studies have proven a direct link between educational impact and learning. As one example, the University of Maryland performed an in-depth analysis on whether people learn better in immersive environments compared to tablets or a computer.[92] The results times, it is an interesting and engaging way to learn new content–exactly where VR works best.

You may tell I am cynical about the area. I feel that we have a few ducks to get in a row first before we continue discussions. The potential of the technology is there, but we have a few steps to go.

The last part I want to explore is location-based VR (LBVR). Lying dormant as the pandemic razed the world, LBVR is starting to rise from the ashes as investors capitalise on the potential of more footfall in the future. Some example evidence includes Zero Latency VR announcing that Advent Partners, a private equity firm, has become a partner and majority shareholder in the company.[97] A vote of trust from a company increasing its portfolio indicates a base level of trust that it will grow further, as Zero Latency VR is already operating well in the country. The same goes for DNA VR, which offers a similar service and excellent multiplayer options.

Another company increasing their presence is Atmos VR, which plans to open eight new sites in the UK, fueled by their expansion goals and investment money.[98]

---

[97] 'Advent Partners Takes Aim at Virtual Reality Play Zero Latency.' Australian Financial Review, 10 Aug. 2021, https://www.afr.com/street-talk/advent-partners-takes-aim-at-virtual-reality-play-zero-latency-20210810-p58hk8.
[98] 'ATMOS VR ANNOUNCES PLANS TO OPEN THE UK'S FIRST 4-D FULLY IMMERSIVE VIRTUAL REALITY VENUE IN 2021' - Games Press.

Collaborations help to breathe new life into it as well. For example, Zero Latency VR and Ubisoft are launching Far Cry VR: Dive into Insanity, a free-roaming VR experience. Games take years of consistent development, and the project would have been in the works throughout the pandemic, likely hoping for a bounce-back more powerful than Liam Neeson's acting career. For Ubisoft, it continues the trend of adopting new IPs for other verticals. In the gaming sector, free-to-play games continue to be a main revenue driver for established players. But beyond that, the IPs have a powerful sway in whichever new areas they choose to adopt; for example, Konami adopted the Metal Gear IP for their pachinko machines. While die-hard fans screech, the money says otherwise. For a run-and-gun franchise like Far Cry, LBVR is a great fit for the franchise.

Will the initiatives succeed? Over 2022, we may see so. A myriad of factors are at play here, but the bottom line is that location-based venues are less likely to attend if there are fewer people on the street interested in having a go. When normality arrives, people are more likely to attend the high street if locations offer an 'experience' during attendance. To keep their competitive edge, locations are embracing immersive technologies to maintain a competitive advantage.[99] Think of the EE stores,

https://www.gamespress.com/ATMOS-VR-ANNOUNCES-PLANS-TO-OPEN-THE-UKS-FIRST-4-D-FULLY-IMMERSIVE-VIR. Accessed 22 Jan. 2022.

legwork when it comes to the ethics and philosophy of VR. If you have a view on the topic, there's a good chance that Kent thought about it before you about five years ago.[100]

- **Kavya Pearlman** – Similar to the above, Kavya is pushing for more standards via the XR Safety Initiative. Outspoken on Twitter, and knows her stuff.[101]
- **Auganix** – Fantastic B2B site covering the business behind immersive run by Sam Sprigg, and invaluable for getting a pulse on the sector as a whole.[102]
- **Charlie Fink** – Runs a weekly newsletter on Forbes, coming from a veteran in immersive.[103]
- **Inside XR** – Great collection of immersive-related news stories that helps me keep track of what's happening in the world.[104]
- **Immersive Web Weekly** – I think that the future of the web is reliant on web-based applications, and this newsletter charts the developments of the area very nicely.[105]

---

[100] https://twitter.com/kentbye

[101] https://twitter.com/KavyaPearlman

[102] https://www.auganix.org/

[103] https://www.forbes.com/sites/charliefink/?sh=bb688244e8 10

[104] https://inside.com/xr

[105] https://immersivewebweekly.com/

You may notice that many of these suggestions are newsletters. I prefer them as a curated digest of news – though this is coming from someone who runs their newsletter as well.[106] Regardless, the perks are that they offer an undiluted summary of the news that matters, chosen by a trusted professional that picks out what is best for their readers. It is direct and to the point, avoiding the sludge of social media that pours out of the internet's orifice.

Finding people you trust takes time, getting your hands dirty and finding the ones you would rather follow. It does take time. At the core of the issue is that expertise has diluted across a massive pool of go-getters, dwarfed by seismic entities that blunder about while legions of followers nod and cite. But when you find the right people, you hold on.

Forbes is a great example of a publication with a mixed reputation. As it runs a contributor network alongside journalists, the quality of the pieces can widely vary. When the doors of entry are open wide enough, a mismatch of quality squeezes through its doors and offers a plethora of differing takes and pieces. Sometimes you get the likes of Charlie Fink and Cathy Hackl, whose toes are sufficiency dipped in the industry. But then you have the rest of the network.

Some time ago, a freelance journalist published a heavily-criticised piece on Forbes, exploring the decline of VR. The article cites

---

[106] A bit like a shoe salesman saying they like to collect shoes in their spare time.

reports that it is doing very well... while talking about how the industry is doing poorly. The language is also stuck in the 2016-2017 era when most headsets require a connection to an expensive PC, which is no longer the case. Experts widely panned the article.[107]

The day after, a contributor to Forbes cited the same article and provided the other side of the argument.[108] Providing multiple perspectives is vital for any balanced argument, but I raised an eyebrow when my search results look like this:

My fundamental problem is that contributor networks split the identity and opinions of the website, and dilute the authoritative power a site holds. If sites become platforms for inconsistent hot-takes, then their trust may erode over time.

The problem persists with other articles as well. Recently the publication released a piece titled 'Oculus will sell you a Quest 2 headset that doesn't need Meta for an extra $500.'[109]

---

[107] Collins, Barry. 'VR Headsets Are Dying A Lonely Death.' Forbes,
https://www.forbes.com/sites/barrycollins/2020/05/04/vr-headsets-are-dying-a-lonely-death/. Accessed 22 Jan. 2022.

[108] Parlock, Joe. 'Stop Saying Virtual Reality Is Dying.' Forbes,
https://www.forbes.com/sites/joeparlock/2020/05/05/stop-saying-virtual-reality-is-dying/. Accessed 22 Jan. 2022.

[109] Dexter, Alan. 'Oculus Will Sell You a Quest 2 Headset That Doesn't Need Facebook for an Extra $500.' PC Gamer, Apr. 2021. www.pcgamer.com,

According to the piece, the more expensive headset—referring to the business edition – costs more because it's 'essentially the value the social media giant attributes to your data.' The article doesn't expand much further on this, as it then touches on how competitors can't match the price of the Quest 2's consumer version because Meta's backing is so large.

The article misled a lot of people, for a couple of reasons. One is the generalised headline, the type that asserts a statement that can be shared virally, without users clicking through and reading it properly, but doesn't convey the nuances of the discussion. No, Meta doesn't value your data at $500.

Then the article barely explores why else the business version is more expensive, doubling down on the data angle. It does not explore why the business edition's additional services contribute to the price. The argument is too reductionist to be true.

I am targeting this article because it tells us a lot about the media landscape with VR headsets. A lot of people care about the use of their data, and Meta's mandatory log-in is a sticking point for some vocal people. In response, publications are crafting headlines that validate their views, causing the article to spread. And the number of times I have seen

---

https://www.pcgamer.com/uk/oculus-will-sell-you-a-quest-2-headset-that-doesnt-need-facebook-for-an-extra-dollar500/.

Let us start with VRChat. The platform had several major benefits that helped with the construction of film festivals. The first is the ease of deployment; creating a world in VRChat takes less time, making it easier to create fully realised worlds for people to wander around in. It also helps that worlds can be built via Unity. The easier it is to deploy sophisticated and creative worlds, the better for time-restricted organisers. My friend at The Ghost Howls points out that VRChat is good because of its passionate community, Unity support, and multi-device support that eased access.[114]

The approach also means that it was easier to add little easter eggs; I chuckled when I found the hidden speakeasy in *Raindance Immersive*, for example. These hidden nooks and crannies add a new kind of life to festivals that should continue in future iterations. If festivals should seek to replicate real-life events, the hidden gems should be included as well.

Another is the ease of access. Accessing the platform is seamless compared to its rivals, where people can access new worlds without the fiddle of alternative platforms originally built with other uses in mind. It also helps that VRChat already has a vibrant community that festivals can tap into.

---

[114] '9 Practical Lessons for VR Events That I've Learned Developing Venice VR Expanded.' The Ghost Howls, 4 Sept. 2020, https://skarredghost.com/2020/09/04/venice-vr-expanded-lessons/.

Both teams at *Venice Film Festival* and *Raindance Immersive* used VRChat in creative and compelling ways. Wandering down the streets of London and taking selfies was a lot of fun, prowling the area with my custom avatar. The same goes for *Venice Film Festival*; entering the festival via gondola was novel, but great to set the mood for the event. When people cannot attend themselves, adding quirks give more life to the location.

My immersive colleagues commented that *Venice Film Festival* in 2020 was a lot of fun. The glitz and glamour of intermingling stars and flashing shoots sparked a fun sense of wonder in my mind. But critically, *Venice Film Festival* has been supporting the immersive arts for several years. I have a lot of respect for that.

When guests pop into VRChat – one of several ways to experience the festival – they slide into the city via a gondola. Michel Reilhac and Liz Rosenthal give their welcome, alongside instructions to participate in the event. Clear and concise, it eased me into the virtual world.

After the trip, I was then teleported to an exhibition hall where I can walk down the corridor with several doors. Above me was a clear blue sky, while a (literal) red carpet led me from place to place. Each door leads to a mini-world, with an experience inspired by one of the artworks selected by the Biennale. I considered these as appetisers to the full experience, a short hors d'oeuvre to the full course. There were two other worlds for accredited guests.

One is meeting-place hosting workshops and chit-chat. The other is for the main parties at the beginning and end of the event.

HTC partnered with the festival to deliver a 100 per cent virtual event, with 25 interactive experiences via Viveport and nine 360-degree productions via Viveport Video. I found it easy to access all of them, and I dabbled in the selected productions for the show.

Gnomes and Goblins was a headliner experience, directed by John Favreau. It felt strange to be a giant among the little beings, stomping around as they gazed up at me with wide eyes. The short puzzles helped to keep it moving along, and jumping through portals to new locations felt great. I have a soft spot for *Lucid*, an adventure where the main character dives into the consciousness of their comatose mother as they find a way to help her to safety. The art style pops with flair and fun, and the adventure made me feel like I was soaring through a spaceship. Another great piece from the team at Breaking Forth.

By comparison, *London Film Festival* featured a platform built from the ground up for the event. Viewers wandered into the Thames to view the experiences via its platform, known as The Expanse, to view all the content. The strength of the approach is complete control of the development process, creating a world that can match the exact specifications of the team. The result is a great experience; I felt like I was roaming around a great hall of artistic experiences, like going to the lower levels of the Tate Modern.

Is there a 'correct' approach? No. Deciding between platforms is always a balance between pros and cons, regardless of the final product. But based on the performance, VRChat has significant benefits for future iterations.

2020 was a great year for increasing the prestige of immersive film festivals. Hideo Kojima, a decorated star of the video game industry, sat on the panel during *Venice Film Festival* to judge awards. *London Film Festival*, one of the biggest in the world, opened its XR strand for the first time in 2020 with a long view to support it in the future. After several years of *Raindance Immersive* and *Venice Film Festival* leading the charge, others are following suit with a lot of support to back them up.

With the additional support comes new ways to access the festivals, via standalone or tethered VR headsets or via websites themselves (for 360-degree videos). While it opened options for people to step in, there is still a general confusion among people on how to access the experiences. Lack of knowledge and unclear directions meant that it was more difficult for people to access everything on offer. Leen Segers, CEO of LucidWeb, agrees: 'The audience is required to… get on the right track to access the festival WebVR gallery. On mobile or desktop, it is simple; just click the URL and your default browser opens. But for VR headsets, there are several steps required to enjoy the VR festival most conveniently. It's a complete new user journey, full of interesting UX / UI challenges we look forward to further investigating and resolving based on the feedback we have received from the audiences of both GIFF and EA.'

Because of these barriers, festivals should consider providing a step-by-step guide for brand-new people, making clear which experiences are available where.

On-site alternatives are critical for accessibility as well. Comfort is everything for VR and having on-hand staff to troubleshoot issues is a major benefit compared to at-home alternatives. While the global pandemic made this more difficult, *London Film Festival* provided a model for safety with COVID-secure protocols in place within the BFI. The first time someone tries VR is perhaps the most important, as it colours their view of the landscape. By making the first go as good as possible, the positive repercussions are immense; something that the team at *London Film Festival* fully understood. (If you wish to learn more about accessibility in this area, I highly recommend this report from the folks at *East City Films*).

Other alternatives include using VIVEPORT and Oculus TV to deliver festival content. HTC has been an ardent supporter of the immersive arts, supporting both *Venice Film Festival* and *London Film Festival* to deliver the experiences in people's hands. Browsing VIVEPORT and Oculus TV were straightforward, and the platforms should consider taking further steps to support festivals via their distribution services.

Festivals saw some amazing strides in 2020 and 2021. *Raindance Immersive* did their first virtual version and smashed it out of the park with an immersive and enjoyable world to roam around in, alongside its (as usual) quality range of selected experiences. The same goes for *London Film Festival*; running the XR strand in 2020, the festival presented quality XR experiences throughout October 2020. In 2021, Venice Film Festival upped the ante and created 34 interlocked worlds to showcase the creativity of the artists. 'I find that the explosion of creativity that is happening the social platforms is so mind-blowing that it challenges the mode of content production today,' Liz Rosenthal said. 'These were people who do not consider themselves artists at all building these worlds in record time. The level of sophistication that they manage to produce in those worlds is on par with the most sophisticated works produced by studios.'[115]

Michael Salmon, Founder of KRAKED and Associated Industries, was a judge at *Raindance Immersive*, and shares the same views: 'I am very proud to have been a juror for

---

[115] Kohn, Eric. "The Future of VR Is Social': How a Virtual Reality Showcase in Venice Points to What's Next for the Medium.' IndieWire, 14 Sept. 2021, https://www.indiewire.com/2021/09/venice-2021-vr-future-1234664685/.

the year's 'Best Immersive World' award, as far as I am aware it is the first time a major festival has recognised virtual world-building so directly. As my fellow judges and I spent 5 hours straight completing The Devouring, a stunning VRChat world that is nominated for 5 awards (including best Immersive Game and Best Multiplayer Experience), it occurred to me that I have never felt closer to my fellow players in a game before. Spending hundreds of hours in VRChat has been an inspiration, so many of the world builders who have been nominated for awards at Raindance are new to game development.

'It has been interesting to spend time with 'traditional' VR creators (we are a few years in, I guess I can use that term now) in VRChat and see the impact these shared spaces are having on them. These are worlds where users live their own stories, as well as the ones they are told, no two trips to a world, are the same. These are worlds where people don't pass on memes they role play and embody them. These are worlds where passionate people spend hundreds of hours building a community. There is a form of participatory culture growing in VRChat that is, in my opinion, the future of storytelling in VR. You just have to dig a little deeper than the sometimes toxic surface.'

While the pandemic forced many events to go virtual, others took it as an opportunity to try out new ways of presenting content. By and large, it worked well, and the next steps are to iterate on the approach to make it as seamless and painless as possible.

These same opportunities persisted in 2021, as creatives tapped into their creativity to make some great new experiences. I spoke to the creatives behind *Madrid Noir* and *Inside Goliath*, both alumni of Digital Catapult and Arts Council England's CreativeXR programme. Lawrence Bennett, Writer of Madrid Noir, was passionate about the role of immersive tech: 'We really set out to make something that is not only fun and interactive but something in which you'll meet a believable and likeable character. A character that will discover things at the same time as you on the journey. The real meat on my part as the writer was to work out how the audience and Lola would communicate. It is effectively a 40-minute monologue with no talking back, and we needed a way to make that feel natural.'

The same goes for topics like schizophrenia; what makes the storytelling different in immersive, when a 2D equivalent can be as persuasive? May Abdalla, one of the two directors of Inside Goliath, commented: 'We didn't want to make a depressing piece, and it is led by the voice of the protagonist. People are represented in a damaging way in the media, combined with the isolated conditions of schizophrenia and leading to lower mortality. We wanted to tell a story that destigmatises the character and the condition. We did it in VR because psychosis is, effectively, a virtual reality. There is a degree where, over time, you believe the world you're in with the expectations you have, and you are in two places at once and you have an appropriate metaphor with the qualities of the condition. Film doesn't truly represent the inner world, with the expectations of feeling. It is palpable in VR that you begin to learn the rules of the other universe, and you're immersed as soon as you're in the room.'

In my view, the most important factor to any festival is the audience experience. Not the content, or the platform, or the prestige; it is the experience of first-time users who don a headset for the first time. The barriers to immersive tech are mostly linked to UX, and how easy it is for them to access what is out there. Designing immersive experiences for the audience is notoriously difficult, and it will take years of iterations and development to get it right. In 2020, the community-made some immense strides. With all that said, here are my thoughts on the key learnings for future festivals:

- **Pick your platform wisely**. I would prioritise accessibility over graphical fidelity, which would already be compromised by developing standalone VR headsets.
- **Build for accessibility**. Design the user experience so that it is as easy and painless as possible for users to enter the festival. Compromise on this, and risk losing customers forever.

- **Add quirks to immersive worlds**. The added flairs add life and fun, which makes it enjoyable to discover and interact with.
- **Test the platform as much as you can**. Festivals cannot risk glitches on launch day.

All of these festivals compare favourably to other cultural events as well. Glastonbury Festival is a staple of the UK's music culture. What was a massive festival where people partied and shared drugs, evolved into a massive festival where people partied and shared drugs secretly? The Glastonbury experience can be summarised by rain, mud, alcohol, and hearing problems that last long afterwards. Watching the event via a TV from home never matches the raw experience on the muddy lands of England.

The same goes for theatre productions as well. Since lockdown productions squirrelled direct-to-TV solutions, so that fans can watch productions on hand. Some even replicated the interval in real-time, to bring in all the realism (without the long queue for the bathroom). But a part of its identity is lost as well; no hushed silence among watchers, or the comforting cloak of darkness as viewers watch the drama.

Lost Horizon's Music Festival attempted to answer in early July 2020, where performers from past Glastonbury's came together to party the night (and day) away. Seventy-plus people performed, including Fatboy Slim, Carl Cox, Peggy Gou, and Jamie Jones. To date, this is one of the highest-profile events in VR with some massive names backing the production. If mainstream attention is what is needed for adoption, then it provides a good kick.

The feedback from attendees was that the audience was great fun. Attending a virtual festival meant jostling between raving avatars, as they bustled towards the main stage of singers ripping their tunes. Participants said the music quality was decent and the festivities were fun, as friends socialised with one another. Perhaps some dipped into a corner to smoke some weed, with security none the wiser, but who knows.

The benefits are clear. Not everyone can travel across the country to watch, nor afford to pay the expensive tickets. It is why so many people watch Glastonbury on TV, organising a social event among friends and family while cracking open a beer. Not everyone can be fussed about coming. VR does bring a fun element to it as well. Ravers and dancers can hang with strangers, who are in turn invested in the music and bonding over a shared passion.

But so many positive parts are lost as well. No waves of heat as bodies press between each other. No scurrying to the darkness to chat with friends or shivering in a tent. No mud or water to spoil clothes or food. A part of festivals is the barrage of senses that overwhelm people, around temperature, sound, and taste. The elements add character. Dispel them, and you are left with a sterile festival.

The same principles apply to theatre productions. Yes, it provides a great alternative to attending on-site locations. Having watched *Hamilton* on Disney+, and the National Theatre broadcasts over YouTube, I am convinced that there is a bright future for productions that have the finances to deliver their content on platforms. Art should be democratised, accessible by as many people as possible to help enrich their lives. When corporate life brings the lifeline, art adds colour and fun to living. Art must be supported.

Let us not forget how technology adds new layers of power to production. *The Under Presents* by Tender Claws is a production that draws the viewer into the immersive world.[116] It questions many parts of traditional theatre; why have an audience to begin with? Why watch a performance at a set time? Viewers should question the assumptions.

My fears are twofold. One is related to festivals; something is lost when watching from the comfort of a home, or in bed. No quiet whispering, the intensity of actors on-stage, or the heavy silence that rests after a significant plot twist. Authenticity is lost.

---

[116] 'Actors Sheltering at Home Perform in Live VR Experiences, Making Case for New Theater Form.' Los Angeles Times, 26 Apr. 2020, https://www.latimes.com/entertainment-arts/story/2020-04-26/coronavirus-vr-virtual-reality-theater-tender-claws-live-actors.

The other is accessibility. Yes, the biggest names would be able to afford to broadcast their productions or make immersive equivalents for a small percentage of their fans. But the cost to access is so cripplingly high that the option does not exist for most companies. Hamilton was produced over three days, brought forward one year by Disney due to the pandemic – what other products could even match that speed?[117] Recently, the National Geographic showed a production in VR live, with an audience of 400 people.[118] While cool, it is a ludicrously expensive option that very few people can access.

A local production cannot deliver alternatives. The biggest losers in the arts during a pandemic are not the big names; it is the small community productions that run in local communities, with razor-thin finances and no support. Over time, the cost of VR will decrease. Capture cameras will reduce costs, and more

---

[117] Pearce, James. 'Hamilton Innovates Live Capture with Disney+ Launch.' IBC, https://www.ibc.org/news/hamilton-innovates-live-capture-with-disney-launch/6192.article. Accessed 22 Jan. 2022.

[118] 'Tech with a Purpose: National Geographic Museum Introduces First Virtual Reality Theater Experience in Washington, D.C.: World-Renowned National Geographic Photographers Virtually Transport Visitors to Earth's Most Extraordinary Places with SPACES.' National Geographic Society Newsroom, 3 Oct. 2018, https://blog.nationalgeographic.org/2018/10/03/tech-with-a-purpose-national-geographic-museum-introduces-first-virtual-reality-theater-experience-in-washington-d-c/.

productions can access the equipment needed to bring their creations online. But until then, only the significant players can deliver their content to their audience.

So why make immersive productions to begin with? I would argue accessibility. While a worse experience, it means anyone can see a play or attend a festival. Nothing beats the real thing, but VR comes closer than TV or a six-inch phone screen. Distance prohibits many from attending events; technology cannot resolve the issue, but it can help. But even then, not everyone owns a VR headset.

Theatres and music festivals have a future in VR. The experience is a step beyond TV, bringing people into the mighty throng of virtual crowds as they listen and dance to their favourite tunes. The heat and sweat from gigs will never be present in VR, but it is a nice alternative for those who cannot attend events. Companies who specialise in it can find success as well, as MelodyVR has shown.

For theatres, the biggest benefit is attendance. Not everyone can come to London, the heart of massive productions, and watch a high-production musical. Immersive alternatives bring more productions into living rooms, and the more support the better. But for local theatres with the smallest budgets, the option is not present.

In mid-2020 Apple bought NextVR, a company specialising in delivering sports events via VR. The technology has its eyes on the broadest audience possible.' That was Timoni West, Vice President of VR and AR at Unity.

Provided that the experience is designed for it, I agree that AR is a compelling tool to use. Anything hammered in would not work. But in this case, it's a tasteful implementation with an enjoyable piece of work.

I say all of the above – perhaps my most rambly section of the book – because I adore immersive arts. I am sure all of the projects will play some sort of role in the metaverse, in much the same way that art has an impact in all of our lives. Little snippets of truths that we whittle on our hearts, which are unique and resonant for each person.

Key takeaways:
- Immersive arts has been growing steadily for many years, and made a sizable leap in 2020.
- High-profile creatives like Jon Favreau saddle alongside indie teams to deliver great experiences.
- Development tools like Unity are strong in their use, while platforms like VRChat saw favourable use.

Meta's seismic influence on metaverse discussions and VR development

Meta's influence in discussions about VR and the metaverse has its gravitational pull.[120] Discussions feel like they orbit around a singular company, almost like a starting point for ideas and discussions. The reason why is simple: Meta has an outsized influence in immersive technologies because it invests a sizable amount into the area. But because of the early-mover advantage and the sheer amount of money being funnelled into Reality Labs, it also leads to one company dominating discussions on both the metaverse and VR.

 The problem with exploring this topic is that it can be mired by cynicism. When Meta's plans are explored, there is an overlaying film of intentions and assertions, where the reader may expect an opinion on the company. I do not. At best, I am an observer who has followed the company's moves closely. I recognise that parts of the company have a political context that could bleed into the metaverse side of the company, such as echo chambers and the spread of misinformation. But equally, I also recognise that the company is also investing a sheer amount of money into an ecosystem where, without their help, VR developers would likely struggle. My stance is that I wish to chart

---

[120] Good time as any to note that all the views represented in the chapter are my opinions, rather than fact.

'Yeah. This one kind of blew up a week or two ago and it surprised me and it's our fault. I don't think we communicated very well. We're here for developers. That's the best way to help consumers have great content is to help developers build a business. So we are looking at ads for them, but you must hear me say 'for them' — it is for developers, so they can take it, they can leave it.

'Some developers decided to opt out. That's totally fine with me. I think for some developers and for some content it's going to be great. It's also going to drive lower prices for consumers. As developers can spend less money trying to acquire consumers in the first place. I'll be honest, I was kind of staggered. People were like, 'You're going to put ads in my eyeballs?' I mean, yeah, it's obviously not an app that you're gonna use if they do a bad job of it. So for me, I've always believed in ads, I believe in great ads and that involves ads that are contextual and relevant and that's kind of what we do.

'So, you know, I get it. People were like, 'you're going to put ads on a device that I bought.' It's like, yeah, like every other device that you bought. People are tweeting me that from their iPhones. So they bought a device, an iPhone, that has ads on it and their TV and every other device. It's up to you what you engage with.

'It's really up to developers, how they want to build these things. I think they're going to want to do it in ways that feel native, that feel good to consumers. Cause that's what they're in the business of doing. We see this a lot already in sports games, where it actually enhances the realism to have the same sponsors. So basically I don't have a strong opinion about what the ad formats are. I think the real key is are they effective for the advertiser? Are they effective for the developer? Do they result in a good experience for the consumer? We care about all those things. And so it's super early, like incredibly early. And the backlash was frankly too much.'[127]

To create a self-sustaining ecosystem for VR content, it makes sense for developers to have access to additional avenues of revenue. Most VR games do not make a lot of money, and act as a passion project for their teams.

In any case, users are annoyed and have voiced their dissatisfaction by review-bombing gaming titles. This makes me feel very uncomfortable, as developers work very hard – to have advertising blowback negatively impact them based on the actions of another company feels crass. On the other hand, users say it is one of the few ways in which they can voice their dissatisfaction—and in this case, it succeeded. I hope that Meta can cultivate ways where they can listen to their customers without having partner studios in the firing line.

---

[127] 'Facebook: Quest Ads Backlash Was 'Too Much.' 2 July 2021, https://uploadvr.com/facebooks-head-of-vr-responds-to-ad-criticism/.

How immersive marketing can be impactful

Ever tried explaining the benefits of immersive technologies to anyone? It's a hassle, navigating its complexities and communicating them in a digestible way. Most people do not have the common experience to truly understand the benefits of what you sell, which in turn leads to confusion. The metaverse is a little worse because no one can agree on what it will be, to begin with.

This chapter will provide some guidance on this. I specialised in immersive technologies for some time, and have a deep grasp on what can work and what cannot for immersive products and services. We're going to touch on a range of key learnings across the chapter, and I hope you find the insights useful for your work as well.

Firstly, let's talk about where people in immersive hang out, with their pros and cons. I've been thinking about the topic because the community is passionate about bringing in new people who may be interested in immersive tech, sharing the love. Marketing-wise, people may be drawn into particular communities – but some have their drawbacks.

For instance, Twitter is full of well-meaning immersive professionals, but they share the same space as incredibly polarising political views and incessant shouting. Twitter's growth is slowing, likely because figures like

Trump have left the platform and its lack of appeal for younger generations.[133] The platform is a powerful way to maintain a community and connect with people, but it's difficult to bring new people in over the long term. But ultimately Twitter is an arena for politics, lacking the tools to help reach new people.[134] And as someone who follows the immersive sphere closely, I dislike passively absorbing the toxicity of my feed each day.[135]

On the flip-side, I understand that a lot of industry people are on the platform as well; it's partly why I am on it as well. But that would make it a great networking tool, as opposed to advertising.

Then there is LinkedIn; a powerful tool for building connections, but feels disingenuous at times. Some professionals tag others to trick the algorithm to extend their post's reach, even if the content does not relate to the tag. The cluttering of hashtags makes posts look messy and near

---

[133] Clifford, Tyler. 'Twitter CFO Says Company Is Confident about Strategy to Double Revenues in Two Years.' CNBC, 26 Feb. 2021, https://www.cnbc.com/2021/02/25/twitter-cfo-company-confident-about-strategy-to-double-revenues-in-2-years.html.

[134] 'Essential Politics: Twitter Is 15. How 140 Characters Unleashed a 'firehose' We Can't Turn Off.' Los Angeles Times, 24 Mar. 2021, https://www.latimes.com/politics/newsletter/2021-03-24/twitter-turns-15-trump-obama-essential-politics.

[135] I also check it every day, which is an unhealthy habit which I am sure fellow Twitter users understand.

Lessons can also be learned from the social media strategies of other companies.[138]

Other companies have taken a different approach to advertise VR software. FitXR launched an ad campaign that uses eclectic imagery and absurdist comedy to advertise their product.[139] The ad prompted a few questions, partially because it gave me visual whiplash like I left a violently-coloured fever dream. I asked Shelly Pearce, previously CMO at FitXR, about their reasoning behind it: 'The style is all about being bold and unexpected to stand out amongst the more traditional fitness ads. Each scene acts as a parody of working out. The intention is to poke fun at the seriousness of the fitness industry and to show that with FitXR, it doesn't have to be like this.' The CMO also noted that the audience they were reaching out to was 'everyone who is looking for a more fun and accessible way to work out.'

Converting non-VR consumers into fitness VR users is hard, but that's exactly what FitXR wants to do. Targeting people who want to get fit at home in new and different ways is difficult,

---

[138] *Fall Guys* is a great example, and I highly recommend reading this article on how they shot into the stratosphere: 'The Social Media Strategy behind Fall Guys: Ultimate Knockout.' GamesIndustry.biz, https://www.gamesindustry.biz/articles/2020-09-25-the-social-media-strategy-behind-fall-guys-ultimate-knockout. Accessed 22 Jan. 2022.

[139] The video can be found here: https://vimeo.com/467798869

and FitXR provides an interesting case study on a different kind of approach.

Speaking of, let's talk about two TV ads that used immersive tech as a whole. One was Vodafone, a UK mobile network, which showed a child using a VR headset to watch a girl sledge down a hill from a first-person perspective. Aww, cute. The other was EE – another UK mobile network – who demonstrated the power of 5G by showing off a city-scale AR experience. One is a great showcase of 5G and immersive tech. The other, less so.

Let's start with the good one. EE presented a great experience created by the team at Happy Finish, using capture technology to show the performer dance among the skyscrapers.[140] A great use-case of how 5G can make streamed experiences like these better. On top of that, the company also created a WebAR experience (made by Aircards) that anyone can access from their homes, having seen it from their TV. A great way to include their audience, showcase 5G, and catch a glimpse of the future.

Then we have Vodafone; a garish ad where everything was red, from the jackets to the walls.[141] There is massaging in the brand

---

[140] *Rita Ora Joins Kevin Bacon to Showcase EE's 5G Service in 'skyline Gig' Spot.*
https://www.campaignlive.co.uk/article/rita-ora-joins-kevin-bacon-showcase-ees-5g-service-skyline-gig-spot/1699990?utm_source=website&utm_medium=social. Accessed 22 Jan. 2022.

you market your company, position yourself as a contributor, not a core creator of an expansive metaverse. That would be like claiming you are building THE internet in the 1980s.

Finally, make your value proposition as clear as possible for customers. Not everyone knows what the metaverse can be, so you need to position yourselves carefully to convey your value. For example, let's say you provide a shopping overlay when wearing AR glasses. Some companies may say that they are 'the metaverse of shopping,' which does not convey what they do. An alternative may be 'we provide an overlay of information to help you shop,' which grounds the service in concrete reality while better conveying your value proposition. Know your audience, and position it in a way they understand without the fluff.

Key takeaways:
- Keep an eye on which platforms to use to promote a product.
- Ensure that the product needs to be immersive – otherwise, there is no point.
- Seek engagement over numbers for success.
- Market yourself as a metaverse company carefully, and do not mess your audience around. Contribute honestly, with as little hyperbole as possible.

Conclusion - A never-ending journey

The trouble with metaverse discussions is that they are expansive and in-depth; an ocean of differing interpretations, discussions, and debates as groups explore untapped and potentially prosperous areas. My haphazard and winding approach to the book might seem sporadic, but it reflects my writings on the space.

As I write this conclusion today,[146] Apple has unveiled their aspirations to focus more on AR, which caused their stock prices to increase.[147] Such an announcement alone would require vast swathes of the book to be rewritten again, as Apple's ambitions become clearer. But if I were to delay the book any further for such a reason, then there will be an endless string of announcements that will kick the book further down the line. There is rarely a good time to put a pin on the story, but for now, this is a good pit stop.

If you tend to gravitate towards a particular area – such as the use of AR for mapping – then I recommend investigating it in your own time. It is easier than ever to get your hands dirty playing around with the tech, and

---

[146] 29 January 2022, a few days before the publication date (2 February 2022).

[147] Kaye, Danielle. "Apple Teases Metaverse AR Plans, Stock Jumps." Reuters, 28 Jan. 2022, www.reuters.com/technology/apple-teases-metaverse-ar-plans-stock-jumps-2022-01-28.

and-snap-partner-jigspace-the-canva-for-3d-raises-a-4-7m-series-a/. Accessed 22 Jan. 2022.

'AR Will Spark the Next Big Tech Platform – Call It Mirrorworld.' Wired.com. https://www.wired.com/story/mirrorworld-ar-next-big-tech-platform/. Accessed 22 Jan. 2022.

'Charting a new course.' Magicleap.com. https://www.magicleap.com/news/news/charting-a-new-course. Accessed 22 Jan. 2022.

'Chronos XR Standards'. https://www.khronos.org/assets/uploads/develop ers/presentations/Khronos-XR-Standards-Laval-Virtual-Apr20.pdf. Accessed 22 Jan. 2022.

'Curiscope and Multiverse Launches Neat Poster Series.' Immersive Wire, 19 Feb. 2020, https://www.immersivewire.com/curiscope-multiverse-posters/.

'Discord Halts Cryptocurrency and NFT Plans Following User Backlash.' Verdict, 12 Nov. 2021, https://www.verdict.co.uk/discord-nfts-cryptocurrency-backlash/.

'Enabling AR Glasses: How WaveOpics Supplies the Key Components.' Immersive Wire, 3 Feb. 2020, https://www.immersivewire.com/waveoptics-ar-glasses-katana/.

'Essential Politics: Twitter Is 15. How 140 Characters Unleashed a 'firehose' We Can't Turn Off.' Los Angeles Times, 24 Mar. 2021, https://www.latimes.com/politics/newsletter/2021-03-24/twitter-turns-15-trump-obama-essential-politics.

'Exclusive: Nearly One Quarter of Americans Have Used a VR or AR Headset.' Morning Brew, https://www.morningbrew.com/emerging-tech/stories/2021/07/07/exclusive-nearly-one-quarter-americans-used-vr-ar-headset. Accessed 22 Jan. 2022.

'Facebook Is Mapping the Planet to Create a Foundation for Its AR Glasses.' Engadget, https://www.engadget.com/2019-09-25-facebook-ar-livemaps-3d-planet-mapping-augmented-reality-glasses.html. Accessed 22 Jan. 2022.

'Facebook Strikes Deal for AR Displays, Squeezing Out Apple.' The Information, https://www.theinformation.com/articles/facebook-strikes-deal-for-ar-displays-trying-to-squeeze-out-apple. Accessed 22 Jan. 2022.

'Facebook: Quest Ads Backlash Was 'Too Much.' 2 July 2021, https://uploadvr.com/facebooks-head-of-vr-responds-to-ad-criticism/.

https://finance.yahoo.com/news/digital-workplace-market-worth-72-150000731.html. Accessed 22 Jan. 2022.

Facebook Research On Wrist-Based Hand Tracking & Haptics. 18 Mar. 2021, https://uploadvr.com/facebook-wrist-based-hand-tracking-haptics/.

Facebook Resumes Quest 2 Elite Strap Shipping. 15 Dec. 2020, https://uploadvr.com/quest-2-elite-strap-shipping-again/.

'The Social Media Strategy behind Fall Guys: Ultimate Knockout.' GamesIndustry.biz, https://www.gamesindustry.biz/articles/2020-09-25-the-social-media-strategy-behind-fall-guys-ultimate-knockout. Accessed 22 Jan. 2022.

'The Metaverse Is a Waste of Time, Effort and Processing Power.' IT PRO, https://www.itpro.co.uk/business-strategy/collaboration/362032/metaverse-waste-of-time-effort-and-processing-power. Accessed 22 Jan. 2022.

Gibbs, Samuel. 'Amazon Buys Video Doorbell Firm Ring for over $1bn.' The Guardian, 28 Feb. 2018. The Guardian, https://www.theguardian.com/technology/2018/feb/28/amazon-buys-video-doorbell-ring-smart-home-delivery.

Gill, Jaspreet. 'DoD 'Agile' Software Development Still Too Slow: GAO.' Breaking Defense, 12 June 2020, https://breakingdefense.sites.breakingmedia.com/2020/06/dod-agile-software-development-still-too-slow-gao/.

Gray, Alistair. 'Consumer Brands to Protect Ad Budgets Even as Other Costs Spiral.' Financial Times, 22 Aug. 2021, https://www.ft.com/content/6367b03e-76e9-4369-bf3b-786b470d84ed.

Hashim, Shakeel; Schiesel, Seth. 'A MESSAGE FROM MICROSOFT AZURE.' Protocol — The People, Power and Politics of Tech, 20 Oct. 2020, https://www.protocol.com/newsletters/gaming/is-vr-finally-going-mainstream?rebelltitem=3#rebelltitem3?rebelltitem=3.

Hayden, Scott. ''VRChat' Secures $80M Series D Funding to Create Its Own Digital Economy.' Road to VR, 28 June 2021, https://www.roadtovr.com/vrchat-80m-series-d-funding/.

Heath, Alex. 'Snap Buys Another Company to Make AR Shopping a Reality.' The Verge, 19 July 2021, https://www.theverge.com/2021/7/19/22583827/

snap-vertebrae-snapchat-ar-shopping-startup-3d-assets.

Heath, Alex. 'Snap Is Buying Its AR Display Supplier for More than $500 Million.' The Verge, 21 May 2021, https://www.theverge.com/2021/5/21/22447150/snap-waveoptics-acquisition-500m-spectacles-waveguides.

ImagineAR's Santa Claus Playing Banjo. www.youtube.com, https://www.youtube.com/watch?v=KxvWkgo8xhE. Accessed 22 Jan. 2022.

Immerse UK → UK Immersive Tech: VC Investment Report. https://www.immerseuk.org/resources/uk-immersive-tech-vc-investment-report/. Accessed 22 Jan. 2022.

Jaehnig, Jon. WebAR Experience By Coca-Cola First In South Africa | ARPost. 19 Feb. 2020, https://arpost.co/2020/02/19/webar-experience-coca-cola-first-south-africa/.

John Carmack & Andrew Bosworth Twitter Spaces Recording. 23 Apr. 2021, https://uploadvr.com/carmack-bosworth-recording-twitter/.

Kaye, Danielle. 'Apple Teases Metaverse AR Plans, Stock Jumps.' Reuters, 28 Jan. 2022, www.reuters.com/technology/apple-teases-metaverse-ar-plans-stock-jumps-2022-01-28.

Kohn, Eric. "The Future of VR Is Social': How a Virtual Reality Showcase in Venice Points to What's Next for the Medium.' IndieWire, 14 Sept. 2021, https://www.indiewire.com/2021/09/venice-2021-vr-future-1234664685/.

Kuchera, Ben. 'The Best VR Device Is Hard to Find, at the Worst Time.' Polygon, 13 Apr. 2020, https://www.polygon.com/2020/4/13/21218930/coronavirus-quarantine-oculus-quest-prices-sold-out-facebook-vr.

Lang, Ben. 'Analysis: 'Half-Life: Alyx' Adds Nearly 1 Million VR Users to Steam in Record Gain.' Road to VR, 2 May 2020, https://www.roadtovr.com/steam-survey-vr-headset-growth-april-2020-half-life-alyx/.

McCann, John. 'OnePlus Nord Launch Date Confirmed and It'll Be a World's First - Here's How to Watch.' TechRadar, 7 July 2020, https://www.techradar.com/news/oneplus-nord-launch-date.

Parlock, Joe. 'Stop Saying Virtual Reality Is Dying.' Forbes, https://www.forbes.com/sites/joeparlock/2020/05

/05/stop-saying-virtual-reality-is-dying/.
Accessed 22 Jan. 2022.

Pearce, James. 'Hamilton Innovates Live
Capture with Disney+ Launch.' IBC,
https://www.ibc.org/news/hamilton-innovates-
live-capture-with-disney-launch/6192.article.
Accessed 22 Jan. 2022.

*Rita Ora Joins Kevin Bacon to Showcase EE's
5G Service in 'skyline Gig' Spot.*
https://www.campaignlive.co.uk/article/rita-ora-
joins-kevin-bacon-showcase-ees-5g-service-
skyline-gig-
spot/1699990?utm_source=website&utm_mediu
m=social. Accessed 22 Jan. 2022.

Robertson, Adi. 'Facebook Is Giving the Oculus
Quest 2 a Storage Bump and Recalling Its Foam
Face Masks.' The Verge, 27 July 2021,
https://www.theverge.com/2021/7/27/22596076/f
acebook-oculus-quest-2-storage-upgrade-foam-
face-mask-recall.

Robertson, Adi. 'Google Announces a New $999
Glass Augmented Reality Headset.' The Verge,
20 May 2019,
https://www.theverge.com/2019/5/20/18632689/
google-glass-enterprise-edition-2-augmented-
reality-headset-pricing.

Robertson, Adi. 'TikTok's Parent Company
Acquires VR Headset Maker Pico.' The Verge,

30 Aug. 2021,
https://www.theverge.com/2021/8/30/22648282/
bytedance-tiktok-vr-pico-hardware.

Roettgers, Janko. 'Facebook Announces
Metaverse Product Group Headed by Instagram
VP Vishal Shah.' Protocol — The People, Power
and Politics of Tech, 26 July 2021,
https://www.protocol.com/bulletins/facebook-
metaverse-group.

Roettgers, Janko. 'The Big Story.' Protocol —
The People, Power and Politics of Tech, 24 June
2021,
https://www.protocol.com/newsletters/next-
up/paths-to-consumer-
ar?rebelltitem=1#rebelltitem1?rebelltitem=1.

*Steve Jobs Quoted Alan Kay with 'People Who
Are Really Serious about Software Sh... | Hacker
News.*
https://news.ycombinator.com/item?id=2763367.
Accessed 22 Jan. 2022.

Stevens, Ben. 'Burberry Has Launched a New
Google Search AR Feature for Its Products.'
Latest Retail Technology News From Across
The Globe - Charged, 25 Feb. 2020,
https://www.chargedretail.co.uk/2020/02/25/burb
erry-has-launched-a-new-google-search-ar-
feature-for-its-products/.

The History of Augmented Reality | SevenMedia. 31 Oct. 2013, http://sevenmediainc.com/the-history-of-augmented-reality/.

The Immersive Wire - 19 May 2021 (News Edition). https://us15.campaign-archive.com/?u=79a59169e0b77435ae7265651&id=c958efa7b7. Accessed 22 Jan. 2022.

This Year, Bring the NFL to Snapchatters, No Matter Where They're Watching the Game | Snapchat for Business. https://forbusiness.snapchat.com/blog/nfl-on-snapchat-2020. Accessed 22 Jan. 2022.

Wilson, Mark. 'Snap Is the World's Most Innovative Company of 2020.' Fast Company, 10 Mar. 2020, https://www.fastcompany.com/90457684/snap-most-innovative-companies-2020.

Printed in Great Britain
by Amazon